W9-AGU-306

50
things
we love about
JAPAN

Written by **Edo Kurosawa**

Illustrated by **Atsuhisa Okura**

50 things we love about JAPAN

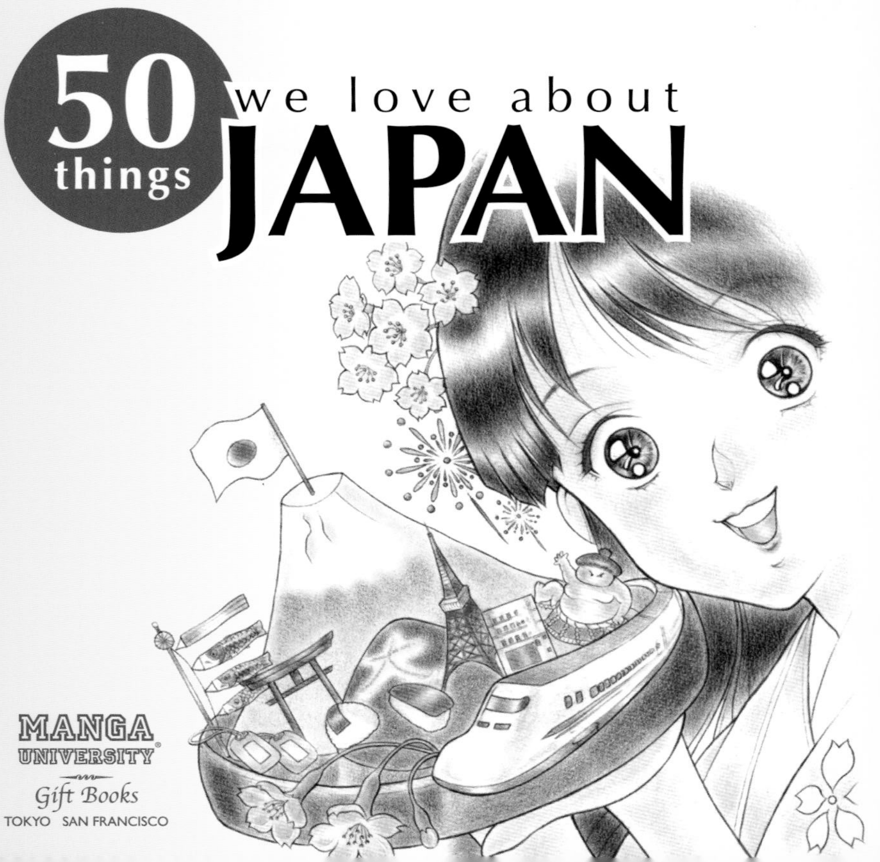

MANGA UNIVERSITY®
Gift Books
TOKYO SAN FRANCISCO

50 Things We Love About Japan
By Edo Kurosawa and Atsuhisa Okura

Published by Manga University under the auspices of Japanime Co. Ltd.,
3-31-18 Nishi-Kawaguchi, Kawaguchi-shi, Saitama-ken 332-0021, Japan.

www.mangauniversity.com

Editor: Glenn Kardy
Art directors: Mari Oyama and Shinobu Sendai
Design editor: Hiroko Takahashi

Special thanks to Mleko Kurosawa and Dale Rubin.

First edition, March 2007

ISBN-13: 978-4-921205-08-9
ISBN-10: 4-921205-08-6

10 9 8 7 6 5 4 3 2 1   y 15 14 13 12 11 10 09 08 07

Printed in China

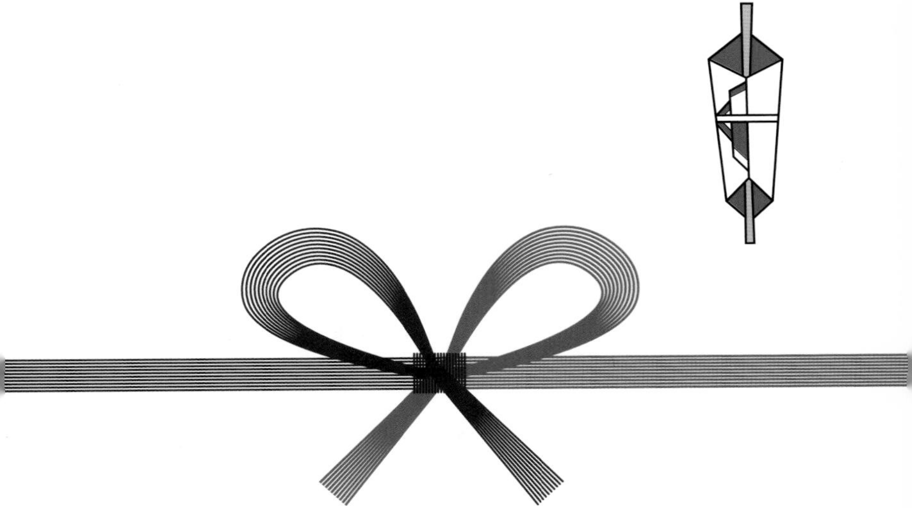

To: ______________________________ 様

From: ______________________________

様 (pronounced *sama*) is a Japanese kanji character written after a person's name as a sign of respect.

Contents

Foreword

There are so many things to love about Japan, yet when asked by Westerners what we admire most about our country, we usually come up with obvious answers. Mt. Fuji. Kabuki. Sushi. Godzilla!

Those are in this book. They are, after all, international symbols of Japan. But when we began this project, we decided to focus on many of the "little things" that make our home truly unique and special.

We began with a list of more than 300 items. Not surprisingly, about half of them were food! We set our appetites aside, though, and narrowed the list down to the 50 found on these pages.

This book reflects the tastes of a nation, but is by no means definitive. We don't all practice judo. Not everyone drinks tea. A few of us don't even like fish!

But as a nation we do have one thing in common, and it's something we hope to share with you:

Our love of Japan!

Notes

The Japanese words in this book are written using a simplified form of the Hepburn method of romanization, the same system used by the Library of Congress in the United States and many governmental agencies in Japan. Words are spelled in a way that allows English speakers to pronounce Japanese with ease.

The Japanese language has five vowels:

a as in ah   *i* as in we   *u* as in soon   *e* as in get   *o* as in old

Consonant sounds are virtually the same as those heard in English, with the following notable exceptions. The "f" sound is considerably softer in Japanese than in English. And the "l" sound is almost nonexistent in Japanese, with a Japanese approximation falling somewhere between a "d" and an "r" to English-trained ears, and romanized with an "r."

Aisatsu

挨拶

Greetings

In the West, you shake hands. In Japan, we bow. A proper bow is done from the waist, with hands that start off straight down. A more formal bow is done while kneeling on the floor. And a single bow is seldom enough: bow a second, third, even fourth time – it's all very polite. Bonus points for bowing while on the *denwa* (telephone)!

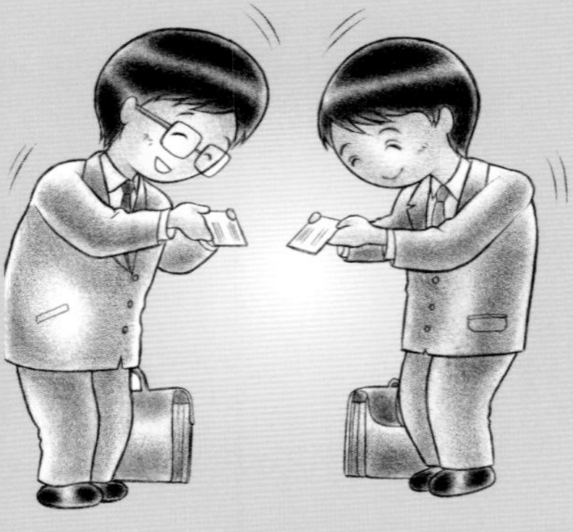

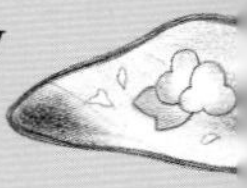

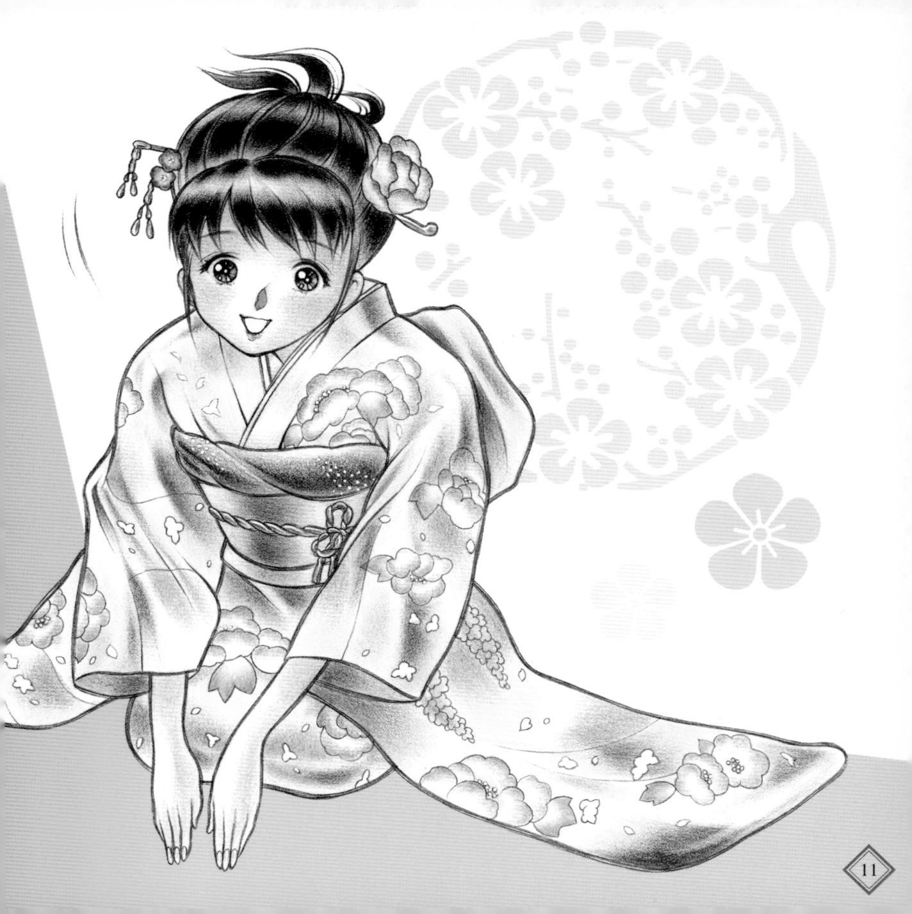

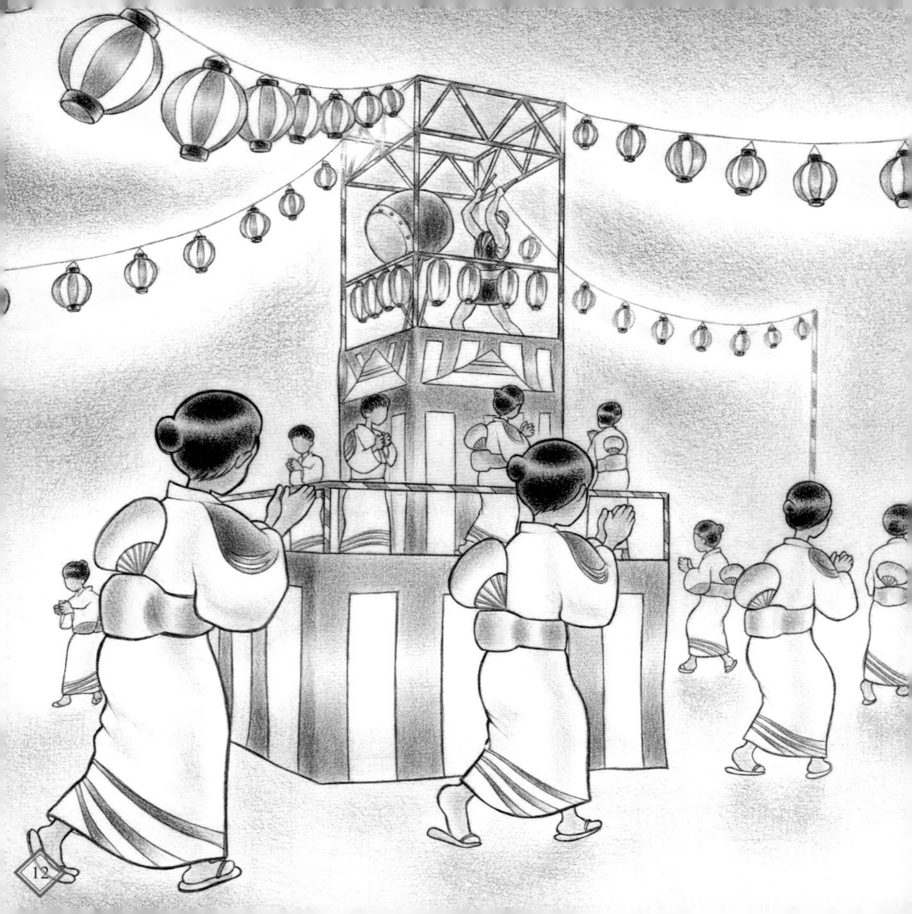

Bon

盆

The Lantern Festival

Buddhism and Shintoism dominate Japan's religious scene, but the most important part of our spirituality comes from our own families. Every summer, we return to our *furusato* (hometowns) to sing and dance as we pay respects to our beloved ancestors – who we believe join us in spirit for the celebrations.

Trained Trees

These are not miniature trees, but actual trees kept in miniature by a dedicated *uekiya* (gardener). It can take years or even generations for a tree to reach a point where the owner is satisfied – if ever. The slow-going nature of the hobby means it's mostly enjoyed by the elderly, but bonsai are becoming popular in the West as gifts. Another great Japanese export!

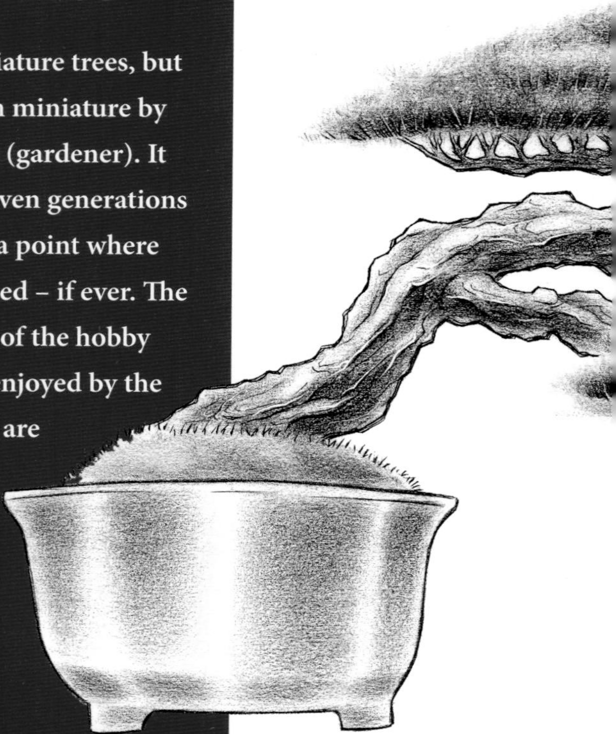

Bonsai

盆栽

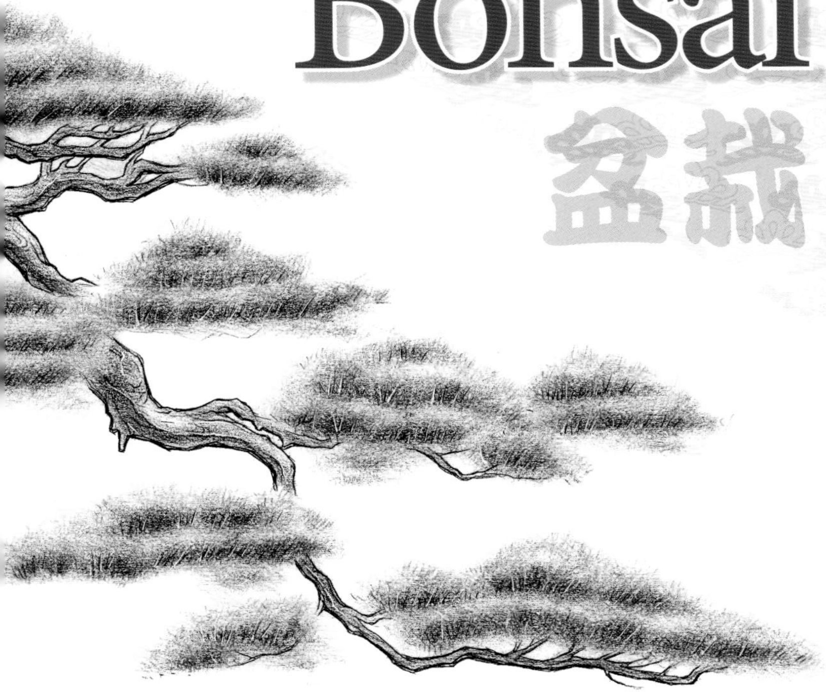

Lordly Buddha

"Daibutsu" means, literally, "Very Big Buddha," and Japan has a few very big statues of the big fellow. This one in Kamakura, a temple city outside Tokyo, is nearly 800 years old and almost 45 feet tall. And if you think that's *ookii* (big), the Ushiku Daibutsu in Ibaraki Prefecture stands nearly 400 feet tall – taller than the *Jyuu no Megami* (Statue of Liberty)!

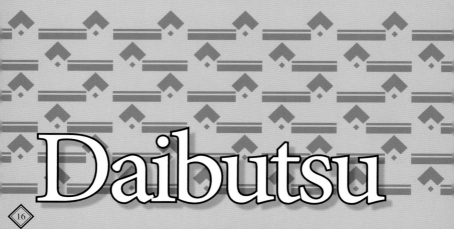

Daibutsu

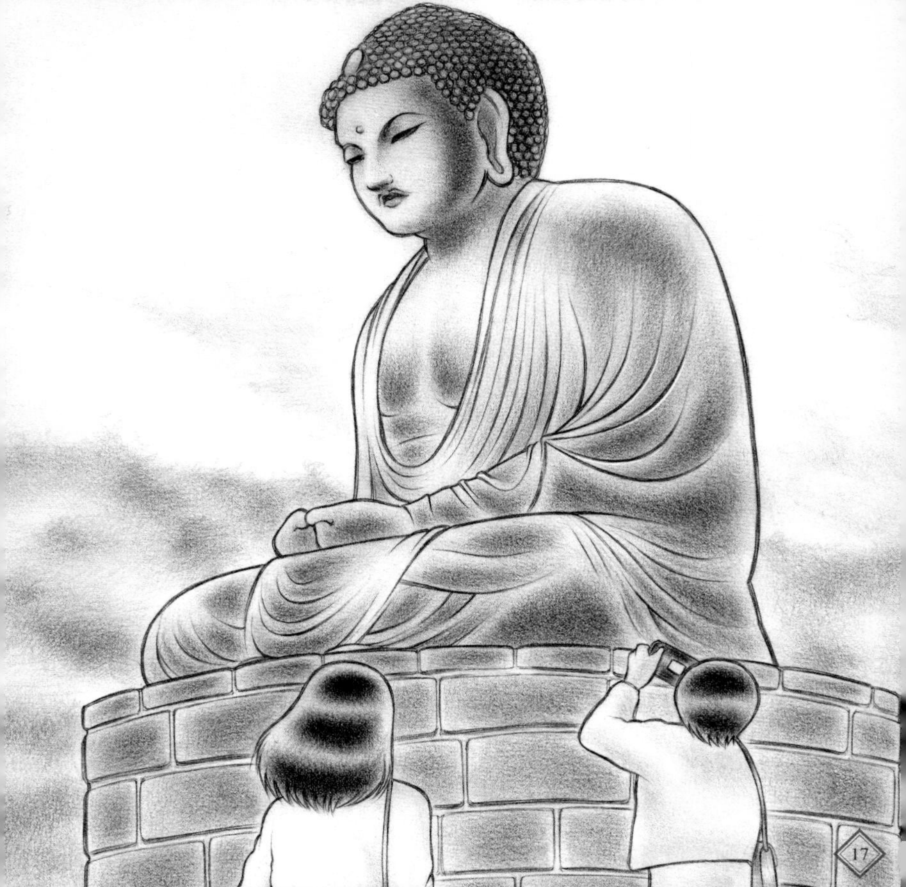

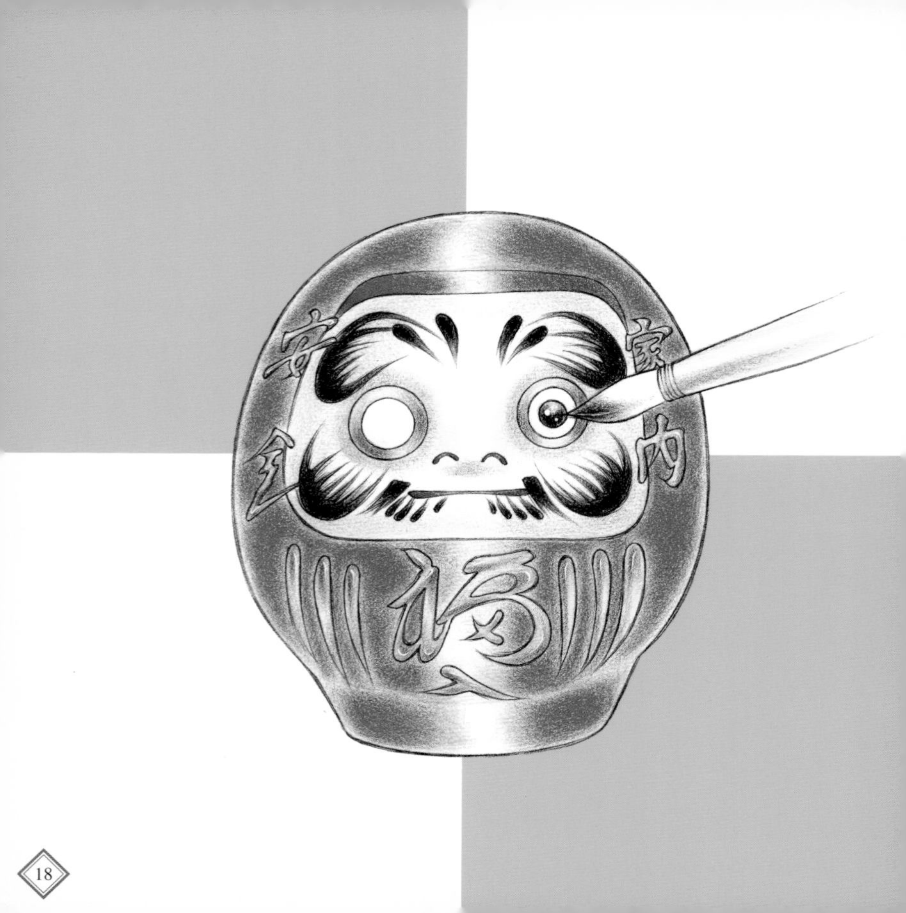
家内安全
福

Wishes & Dolls

Buy one of these dolls, and as you make a wish or set a goal, paint in one *me* (eye). When your wish comes true, fill in the second eye. Politicians generally paint in one eye when running for office – and the second eye when they win. Daruma can be bought in stores, but it's more fun to purchase them at temples.

Daruma

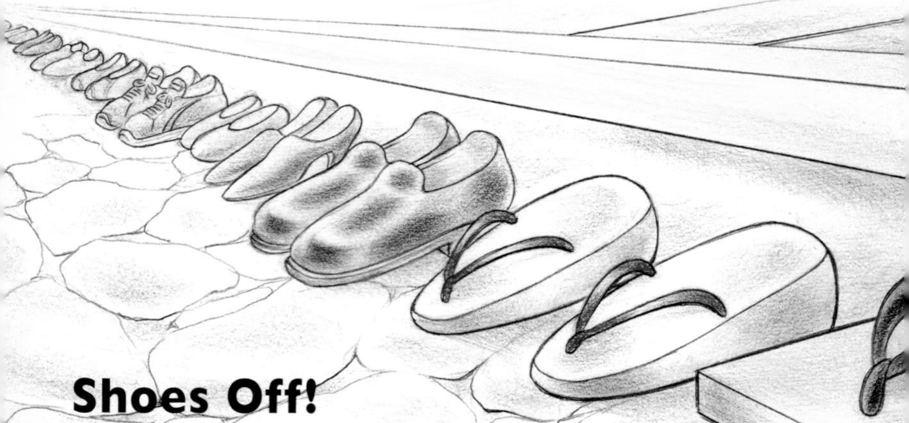

Shoes Off!

We always take off our footwear before we enter a Japanese home, temple, school, or any one of a number of places. Even some restaurants ban shoes. Why? Think of everything you stepped in today. Then think of everything you may have stepped in without even realizing it. Would you really want that inside with you? In Japan, much eating and sleeping is still done on straw-mat floors, providing extra incentive to leave the *kutsu* (shoes) outside. Maybe you should try it too!

土足厳禁

Dosoku-genkin

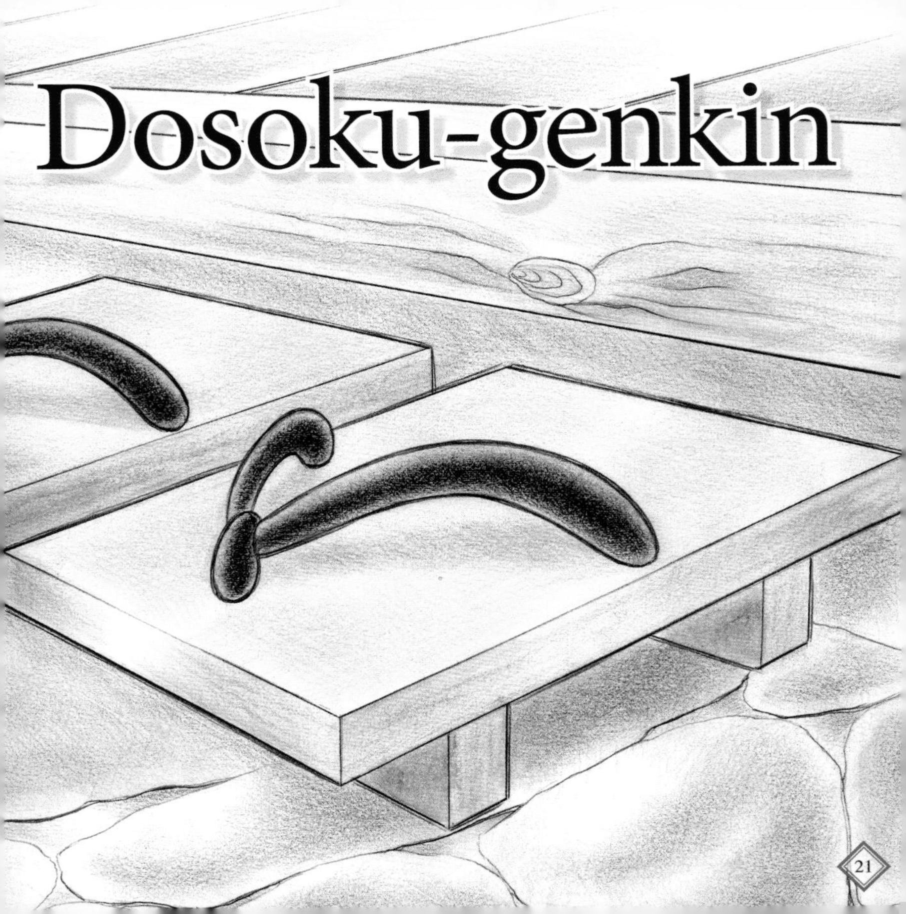

Go & Shogi

碁と将棋

Games of Skill

Both of these games are considered a kind of chess in Japan. Shogi is perhaps closer to traditional chess, with somewhat complex rules and different kinds of pieces that move in different ways. Go is very simple: place your *goishi* (stones) onto the board, try to surround your opponent's stones and capture his territory. Simple to learn – but difficult to master.

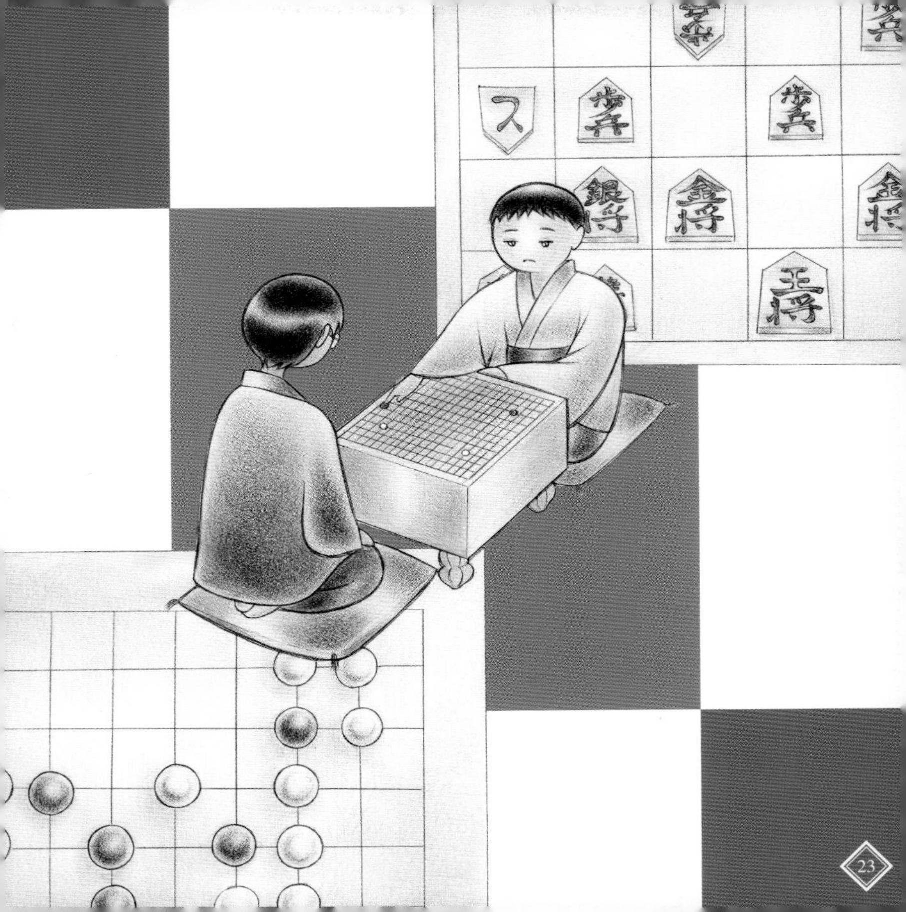
歩兵
歩兵
銀将
金将
王将

Shibuya's Best Friend

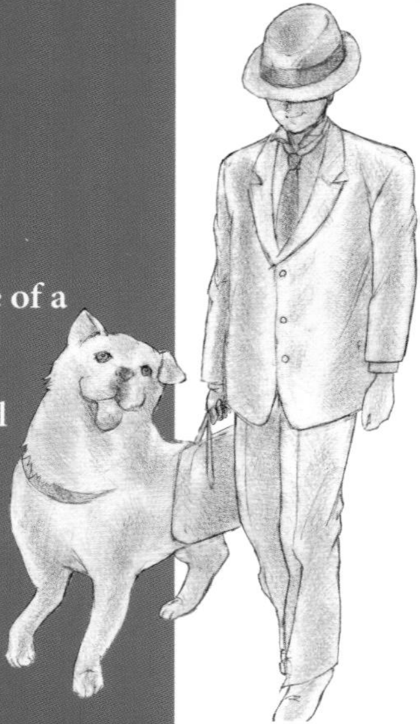

Where else would a statue of a cute little *inu* (dog) get so much love? Just as the real Hachiko would faithfully wait at Tokyo's Shibuya Station for his master to arrive home from work each evening – even years after the man died – so do young friends and lovers wait faithfully for one another under the statue today.

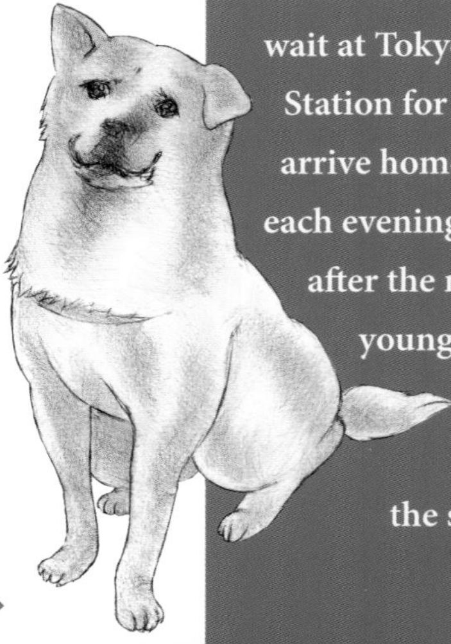

Hachiko

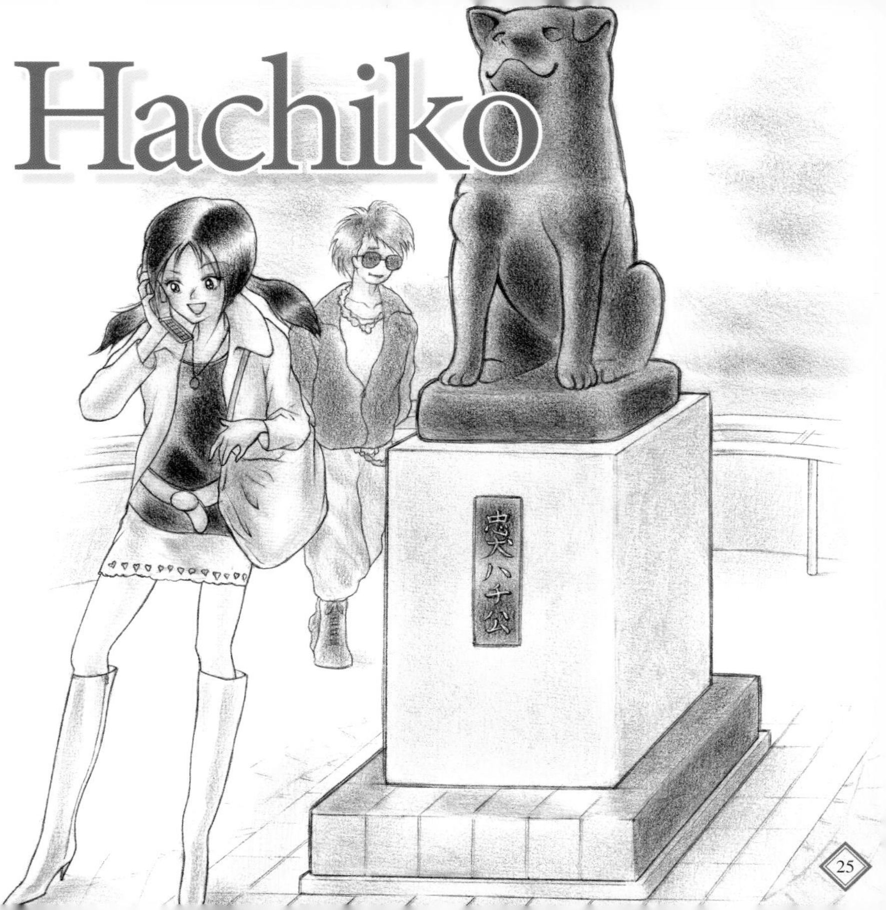
忠犬ハチ公

Lighting the Night

You simply can't have a festival in Japan without fireworks. And since festivals happen throughout the year, one might stumble upon a spectacular display on any given night. The biggest hanabi show of all is held over the Sumida River in Tokyo during the summer. As the rockets explode, we shout "Tamaya!" and "Kagiya!" in honor of the two rival fireworks companies that started the festival nearly 300 years ago.

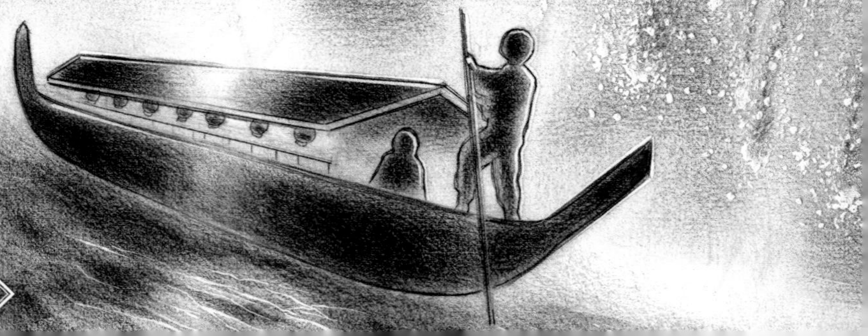

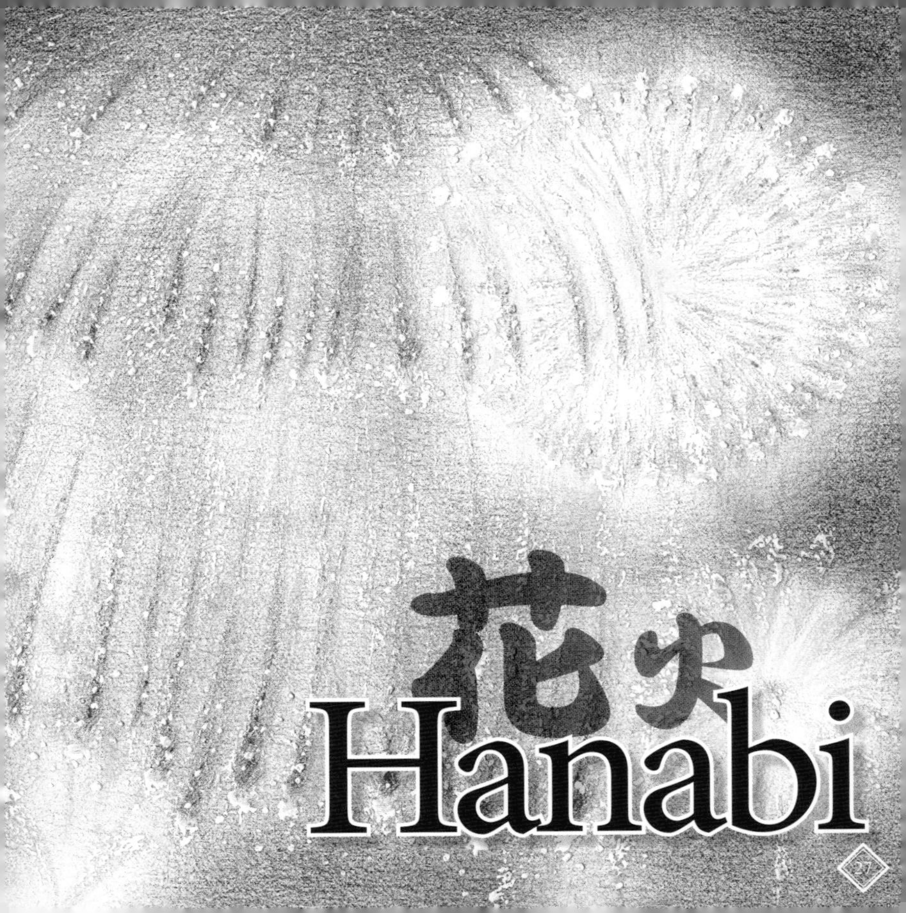

花火
Hanabi

花札

Flower Cards

These cards are used by gamblers, but they're made by artists. Each card is a true work of art in miniature. Hanafuda decks feature a dozen suits of four cards each, so there is more variety than in a Western deck. The most popular hanafuda game is *koi-koi*, a type of matching game.

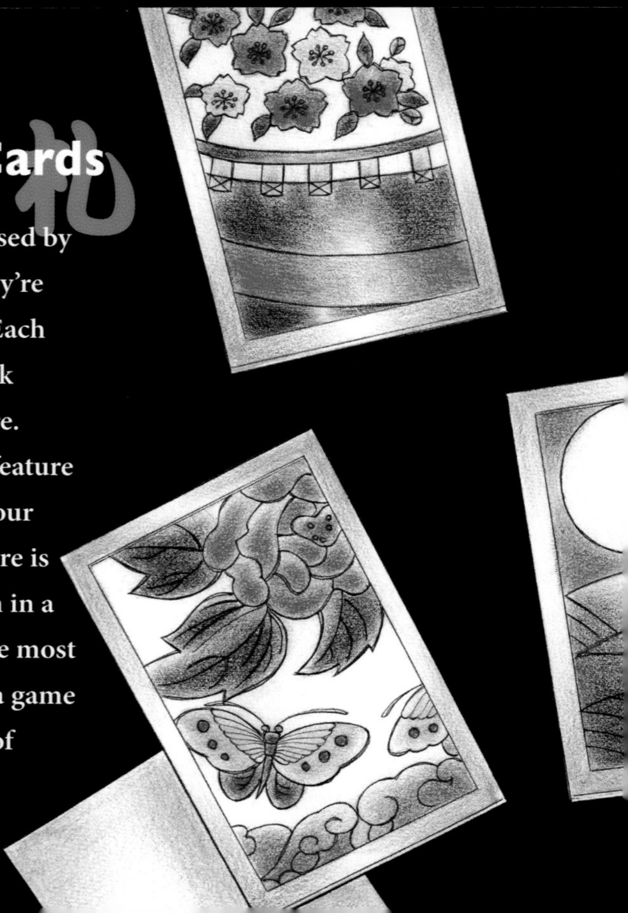

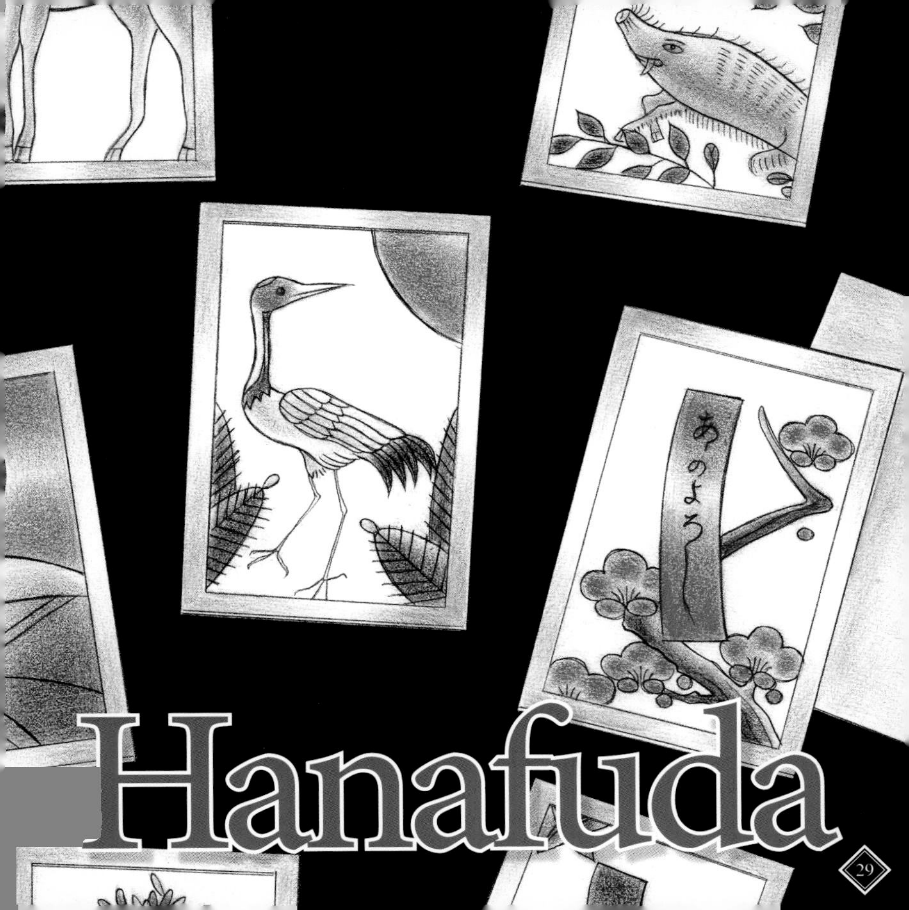
あのよろし

Hanafuda

Hinamatsuri

Girls & Dolls

This festival celebrates girls, who display their *hina* dolls in late winter. But these aren't your typical Kens and Barbies. They depict an emperor and empress and their royal court – and can be quite elaborate. Many are displayed in a glass case. We must be sure to put the dolls away by March 3, the day of the festival, though. Legend has it our daughters will become spinsters if we don't!

雛祭り

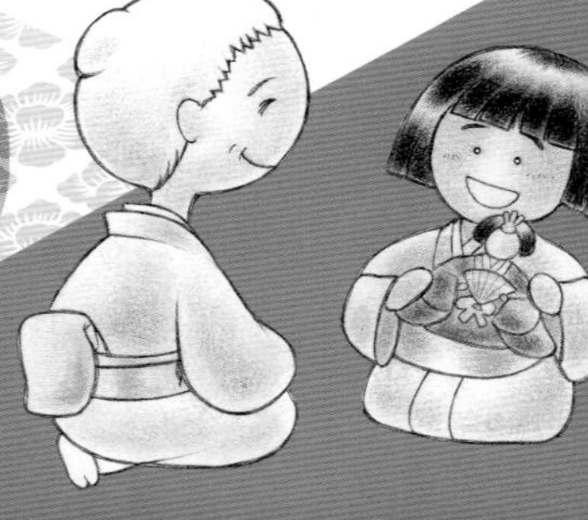

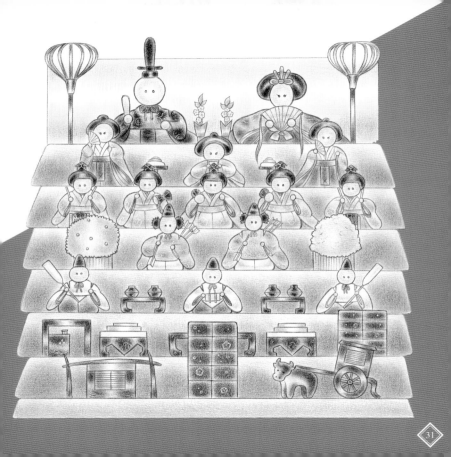

自動販売機

Store in a Box

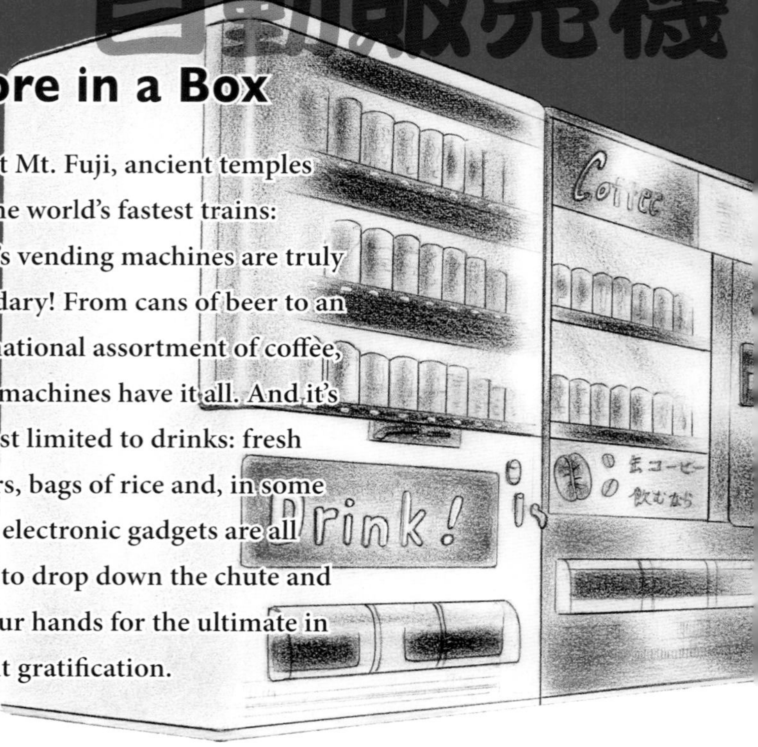
Coffee
缶コーヒー
飲むなら
Drink!

Forget Mt. Fuji, ancient temples and the world's fastest trains: Japan's vending machines are truly legendary! From cans of beer to an international assortment of coffee, these machines have it all. And it's not just limited to drinks: fresh flowers, bags of rice and, in some cases, electronic gadgets are all ready to drop down the chute and into our hands for the ultimate in instant gratification.

And if we forgot our cash, we can even use our *keitai* (cellular phone) to pay!

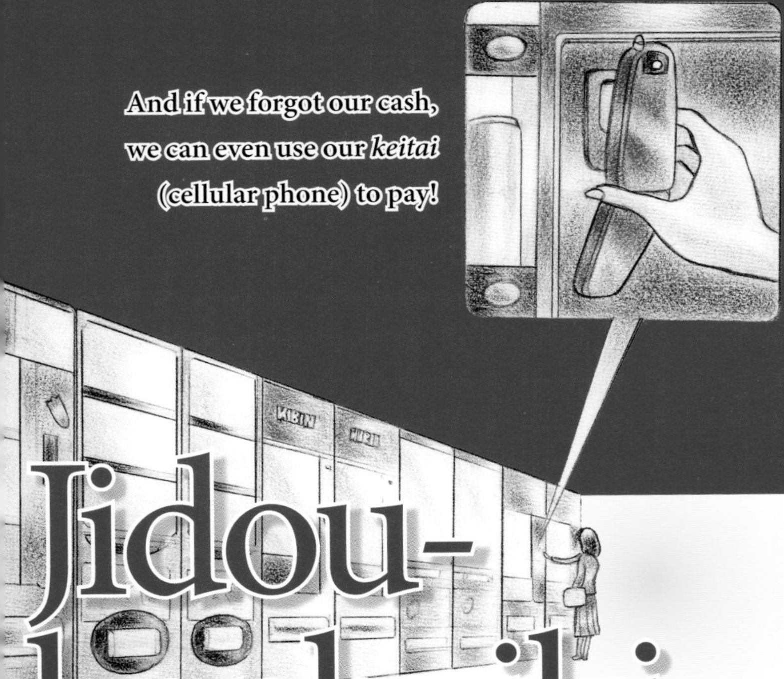

Jidou-hanbaiki

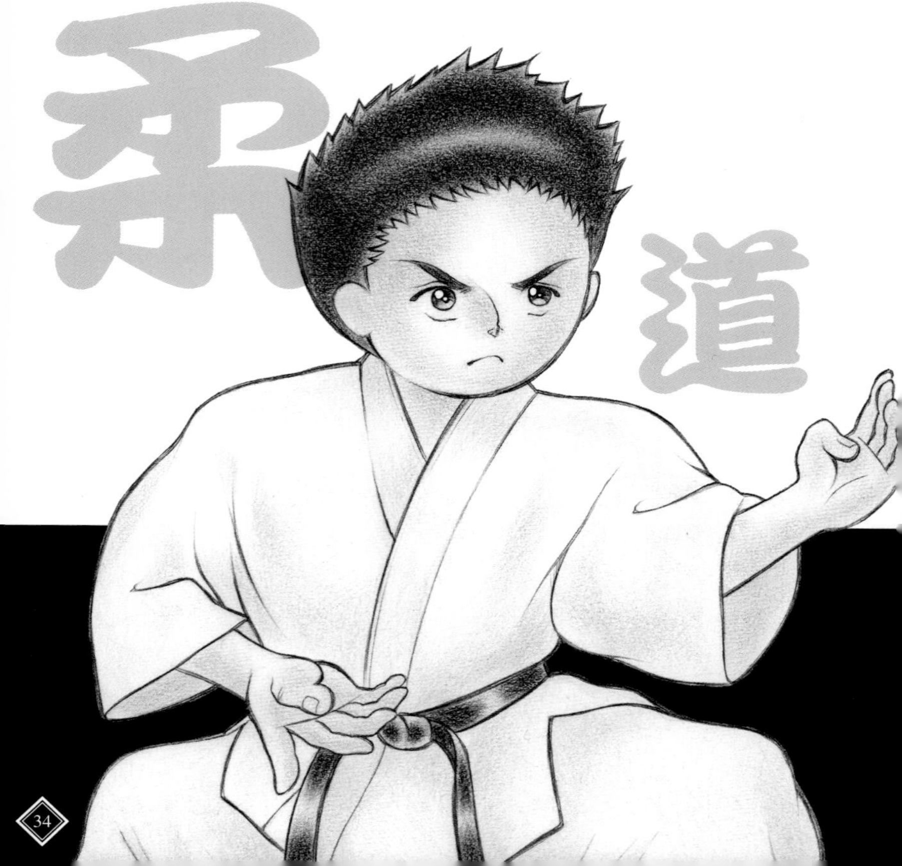
柔
道

The Gentle Way

Many kinds of marital arts are practiced in Japan, but judo has a special place in our hearts. In 1882, Dr. Jigoro Kano took a number of ancient martial arts then known as *jujutsu* and created judo. The main principle is to use an opponent's own force and momentum against him. But judo requires more than just physical prowess; there is a strong mental component as well.

Judo

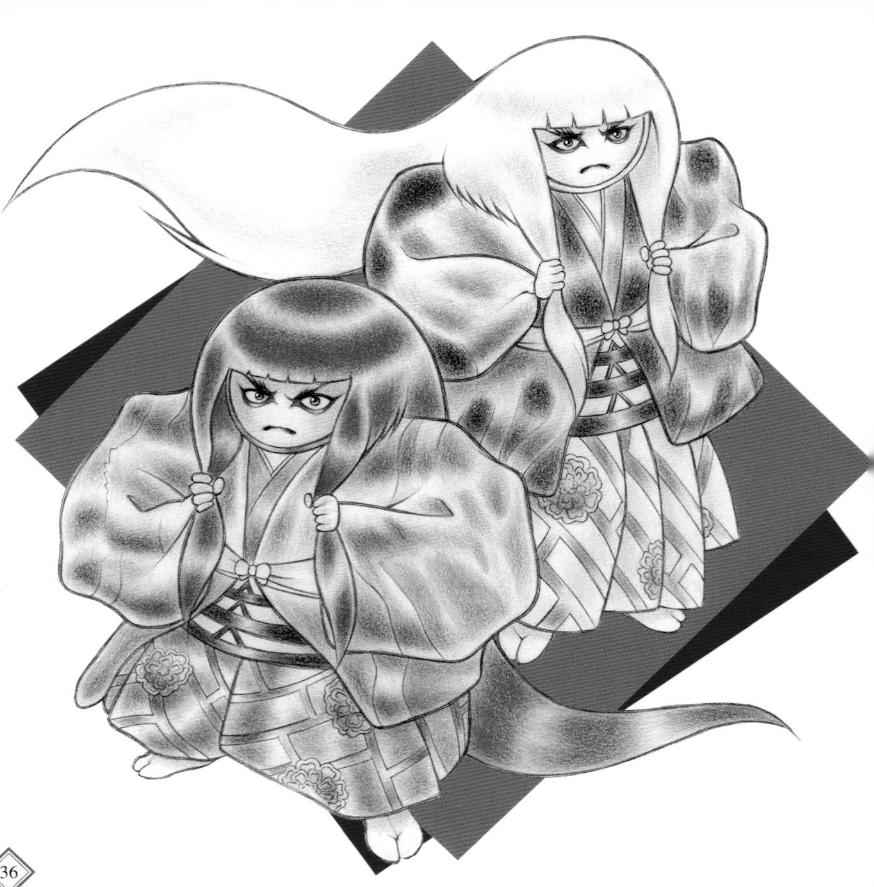

Kabuki

歌舞伎

Costume Play

If noh is the cultured equivalent of high theater, kabuki is theater for the masses. Hundreds of years older than Broadway, kabuki plays feature singing, dancing, drama – and a certain amount of audience participation. Fans offer shouts of encouragement, called *kakegoe*, at the actors, most of whom are men – but it can be hard to tell beneath the makeup, wigs, armor and the rest of the elaborate wardrobe.

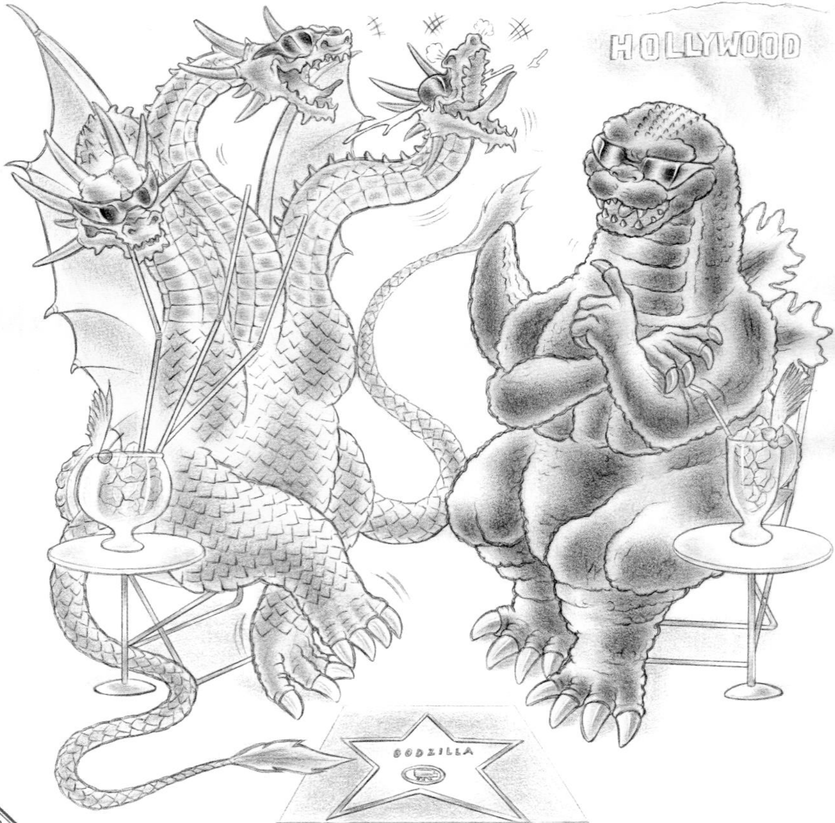
HOLLYWOOD
GODZILLA

Monster Mash

Oh no! There goes Tokyo!
The biggest brawlers in Japan
aren't sumo wrestlers. Those
guys are positively tiny compared to the
building-bashing movie monsters we call
kaiju. Who cares if they look exactly like men in
rubber suits stomping on plastic models – pop culture
throughout the world wouldn't be the same without
our radioactive lizards, giant insects and
multi-headed alien beasts.

Kaiju

怪獣

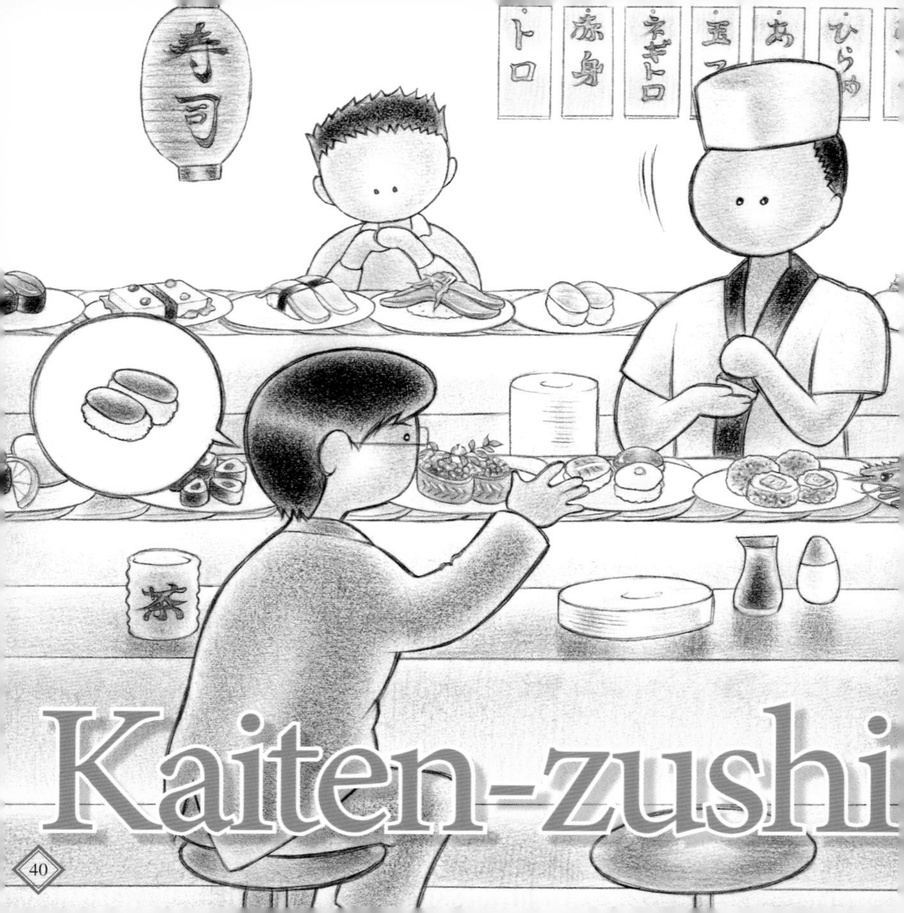
寿司
トロ
赤身
ネギトロ
茶

Kaiten-zushi

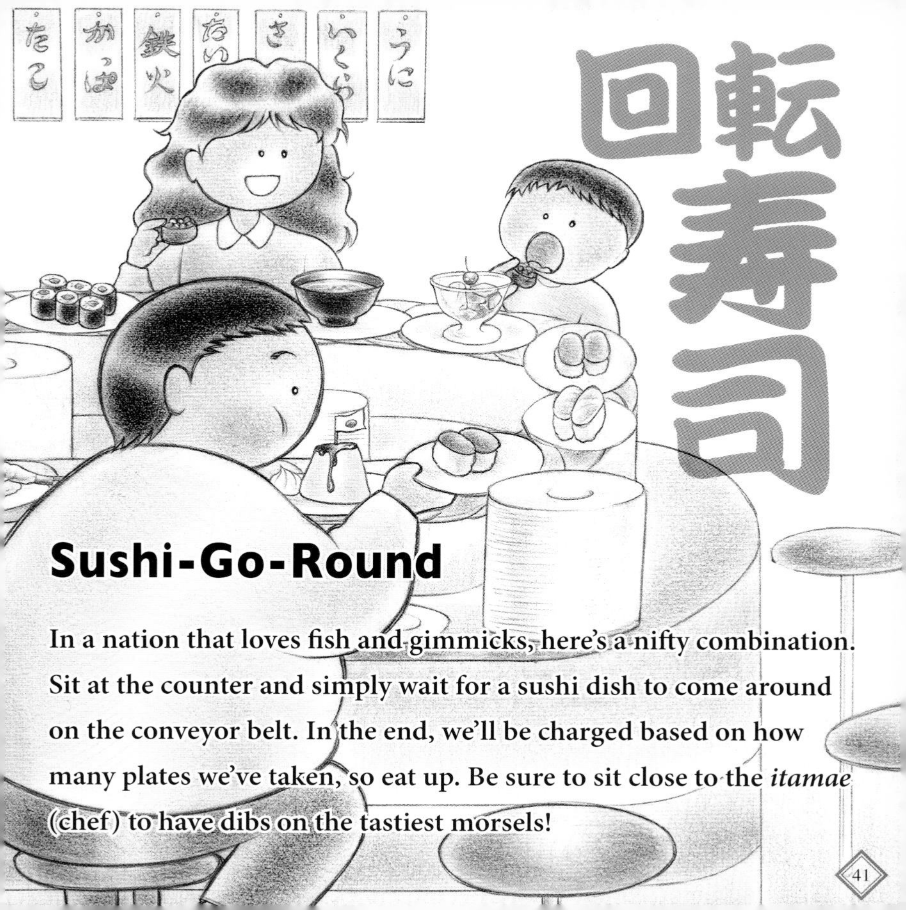
たこ
かっぱ
鉄火
たい
さ
いくら
うに

回転寿司

Sushi-Go-Round

In a nation that loves fish and gimmicks, here's a nifty combination. Sit at the counter and simply wait for a sushi dish to come around on the conveyor belt. In the end, we'll be charged based on how many plates we've taken, so eat up. Be sure to sit close to the *itamae* (chef) to have dibs on the tastiest morsels!

Wedding Vows

結婚式

Everyone loves a wedding, and we Japanese are no exception. While many choose what looks much like a Western Christian service, traditional weddings in Japan are Shinto affairs.

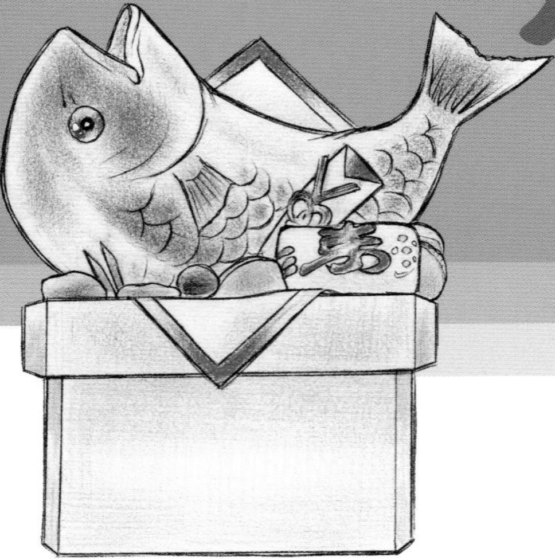

And forget the bridal registry – our weddings are largely cash affairs, the amount based on one's relationship to the happy *fuufu* (couple).

Kekkon-shiki

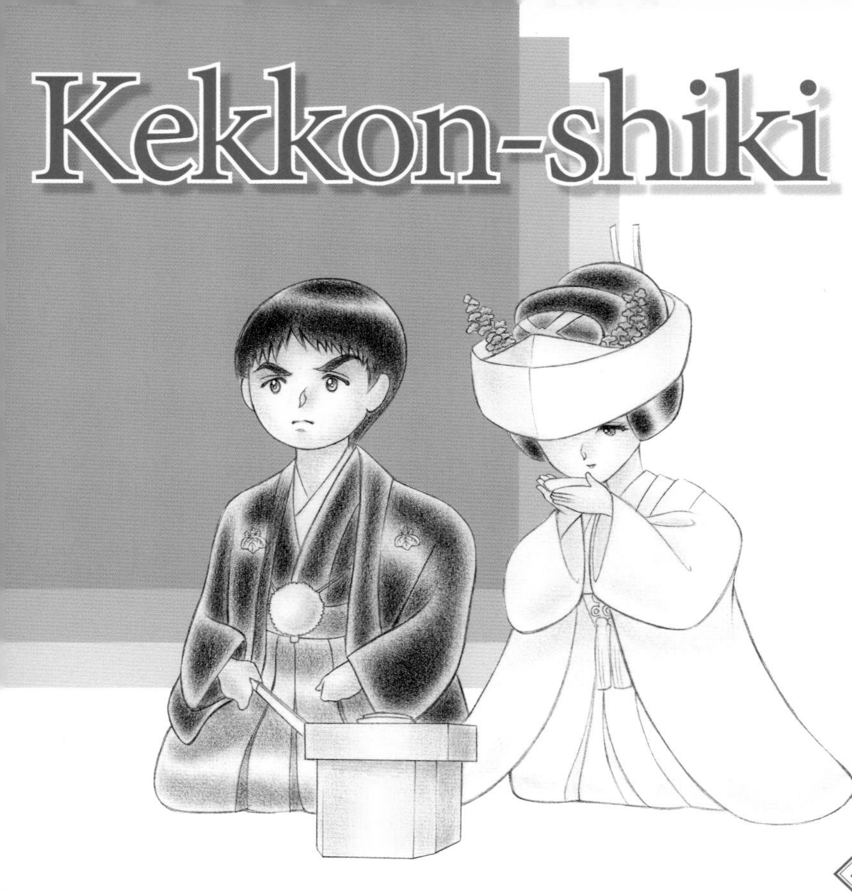

To Protect and Serve

Community policing is in full force – even in Japan's biggest cities. There is always a koban – police box – nearby, where we can go for anything from reporting a lost wallet to getting directions to the nearest gas station. And a kind *omawarisan* (police officer) is more than willing to help an *obaasan* (grandma) cross the street.

交番

Koban

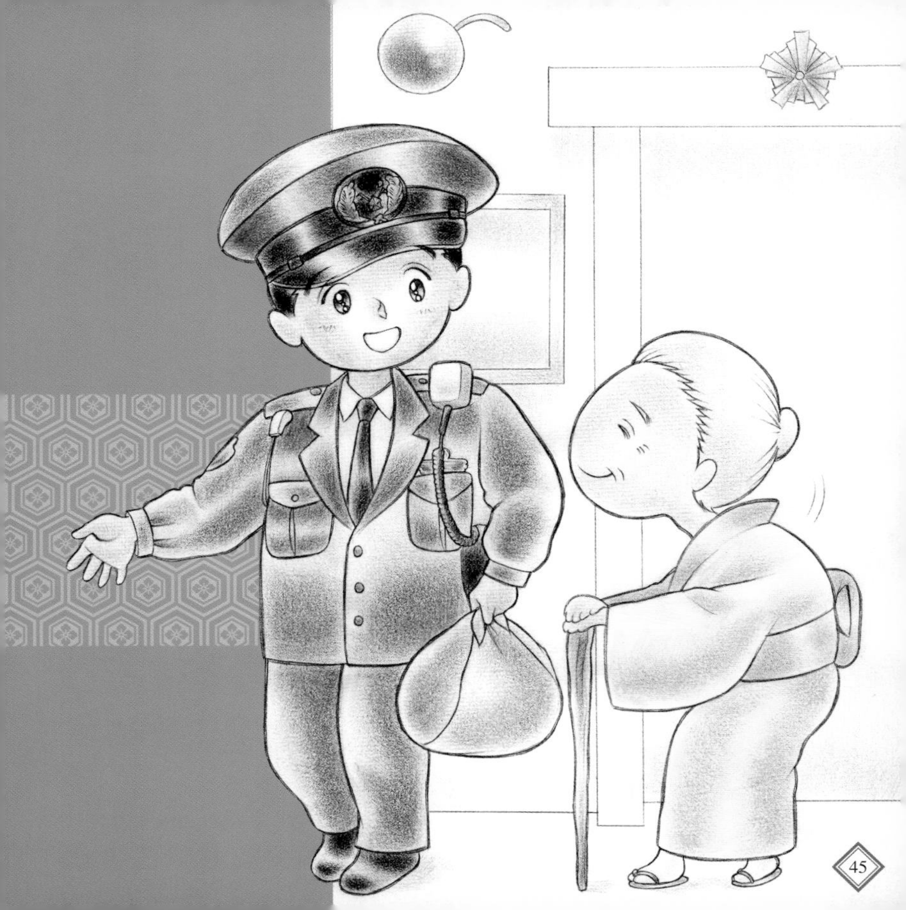

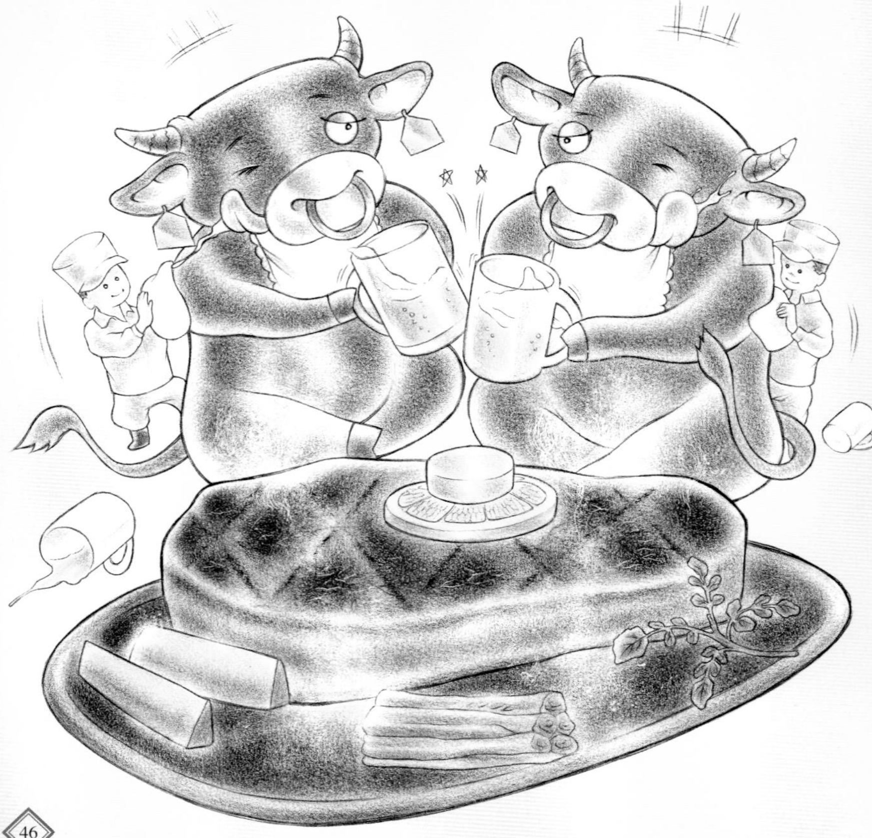

Kobe Beef 神戸牛

Beef at its Best

If you think the Japanese are particular when it comes to seafood, you should see what we expect from our beef! Of all the varieties of *wagyu* (Japanese beef), Kobe beef is the most famous – and most expensive. The cattle are fed beer to fatten them up and massaged to keep them tender. In the end, the meat has a very distinct marbling pattern – and an even more distinctive price tag!

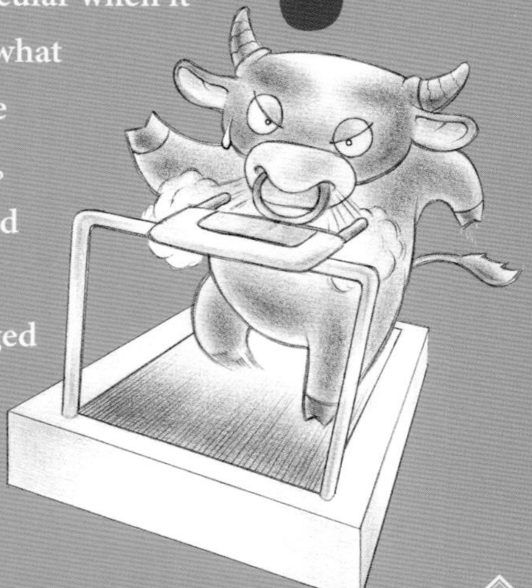

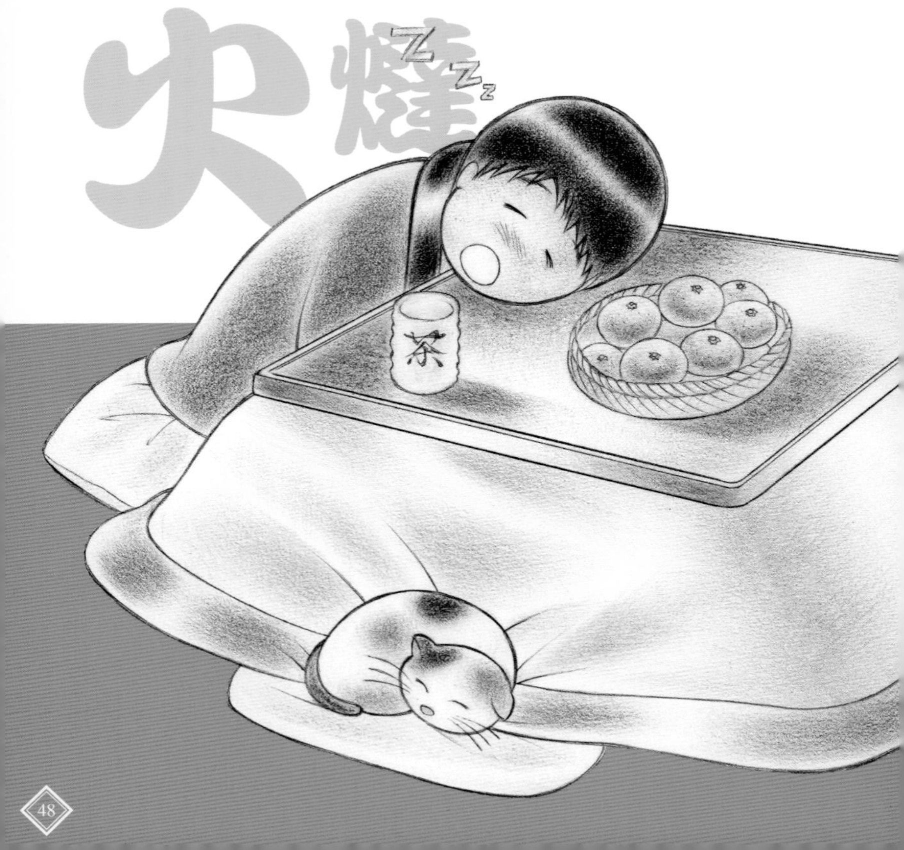
火燵
Zzz
茶

Kotatsu

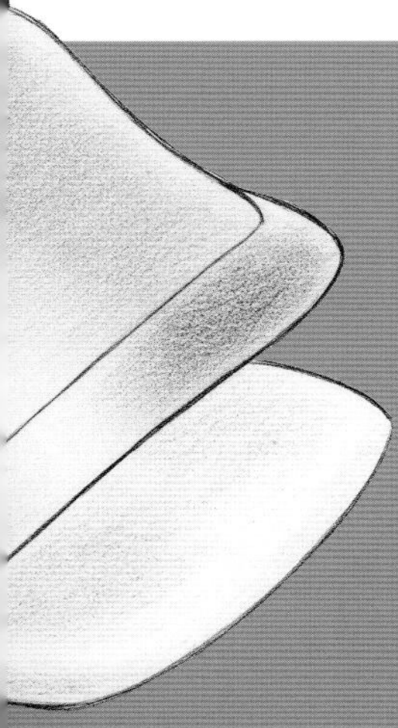

Winter Warm-up

Many Japanese homes and apartments are without central heating, so keeping warm in winter requires a little ingenuity. Enter the kotatsu. It looks like a little coffee table. But when the mercury drops, we plug it in, attach a special *futon* (blanket), and the table's built-in heater keeps us as snug as can be.

Imperial City

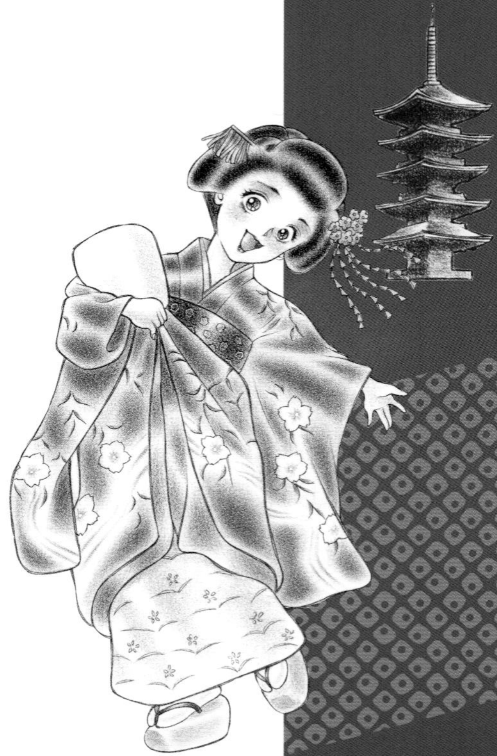

Japan's ancient capital is full of amazing temples, and its citizenry is steeped in the city's rich culture. Here we have a *maikosan*, a traditional dancing girl. A bonfire festival leaves the kanji character 大 (big) burned into the side of a hill overlooking the city and the 700-year-old Golden Pavilion, which is covered in gold leaf. Kyoto beckons!

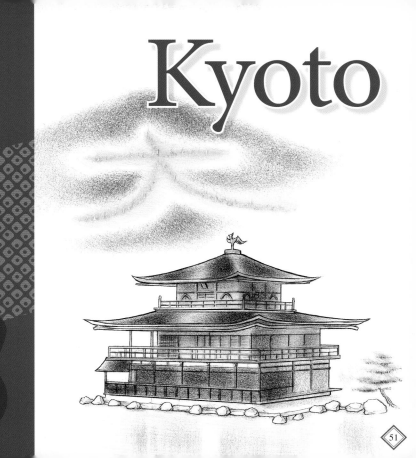

Kyoto

Money Cat

This little ceramic kitty helps bring good fortune to businesses. Her paw is raised in the Japanese gesture for "come on over," and shopkeepers hope she'll attract *okyakusama* (customers) – and their *okane* (money). Manekineko are also common as a Japanese version of a piggy bank.

Manekineko

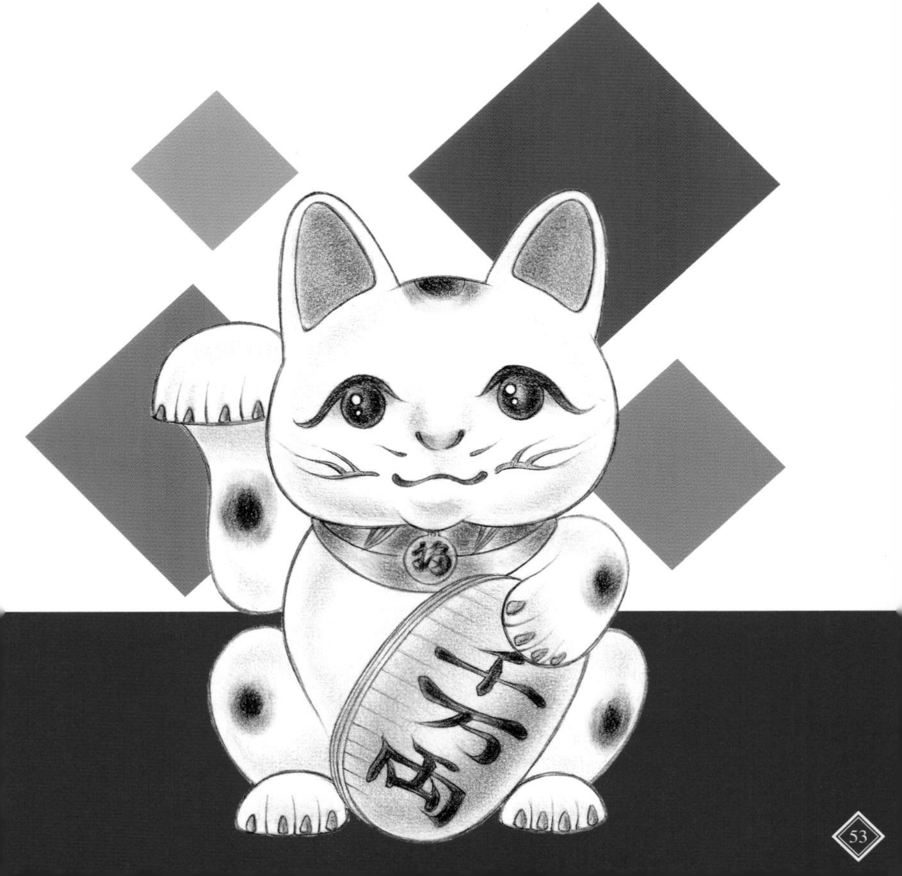
福
千万両

神輿

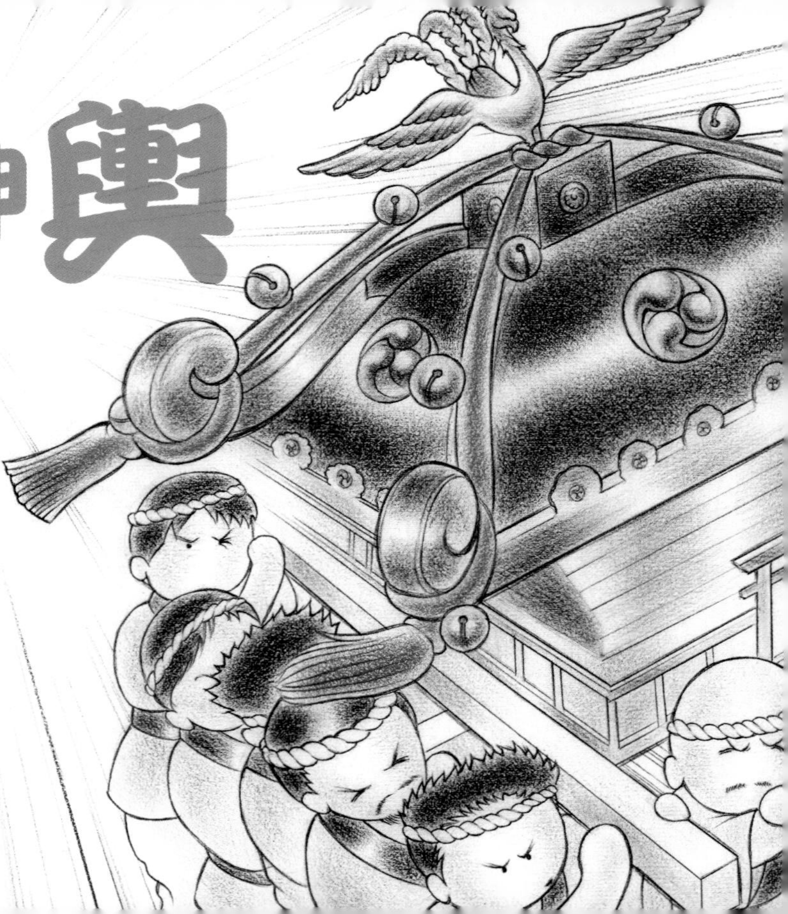

Mikoshi

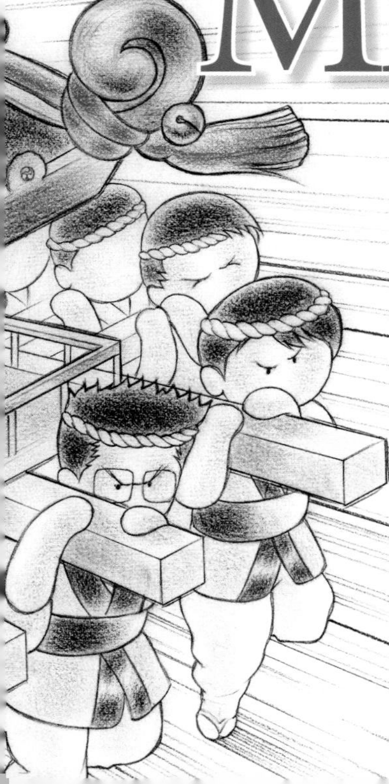

Chariots of the Gods

In Japan, we don't always have to go to the shrine – sometimes, the shrine comes to us! Mikoshi are portable Shinto shrines used during festivals. But the *kami* (deities) rarely ride in comfort – the faithful keep the spirits amused by bouncing the mikoshi up and down and carrying it in a crazy zig-zag pattern.

Majestic Mountain

The perfect cone of Mt. Fuji is more than just a postcard: it's a symbol of the country, a national treasure. Fujisan, as we call it in Japanese, is also a volcano – a dormant one, but certainly not an extinct one. Hikers climb the 12,388-foot mountain throughout the summer and into early autumn.

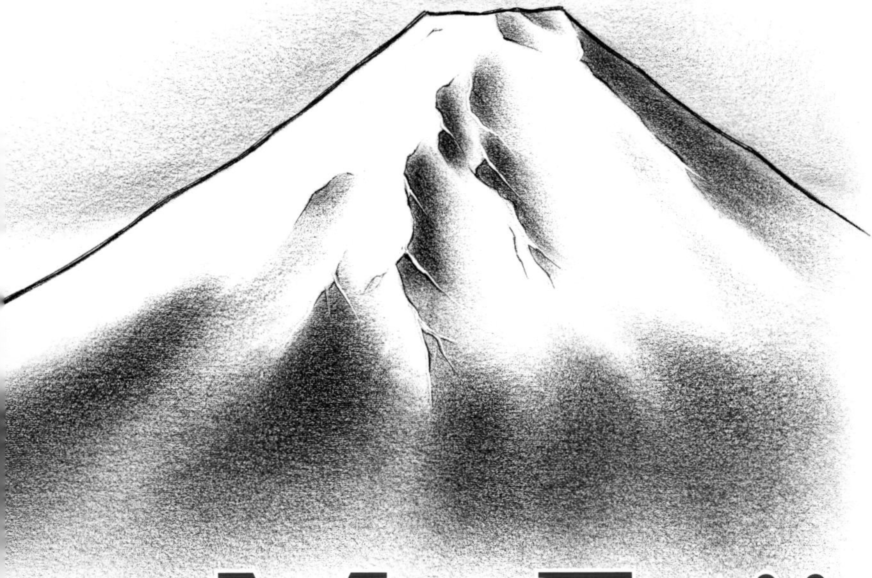

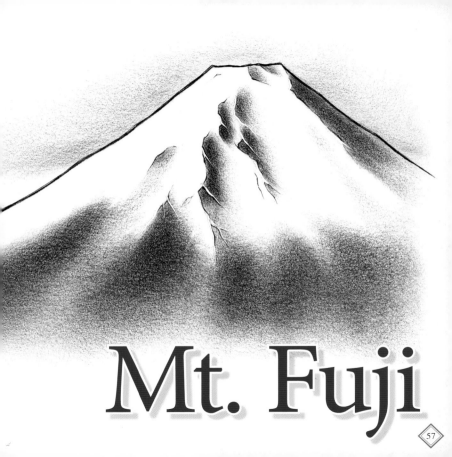

Mt. Fuji

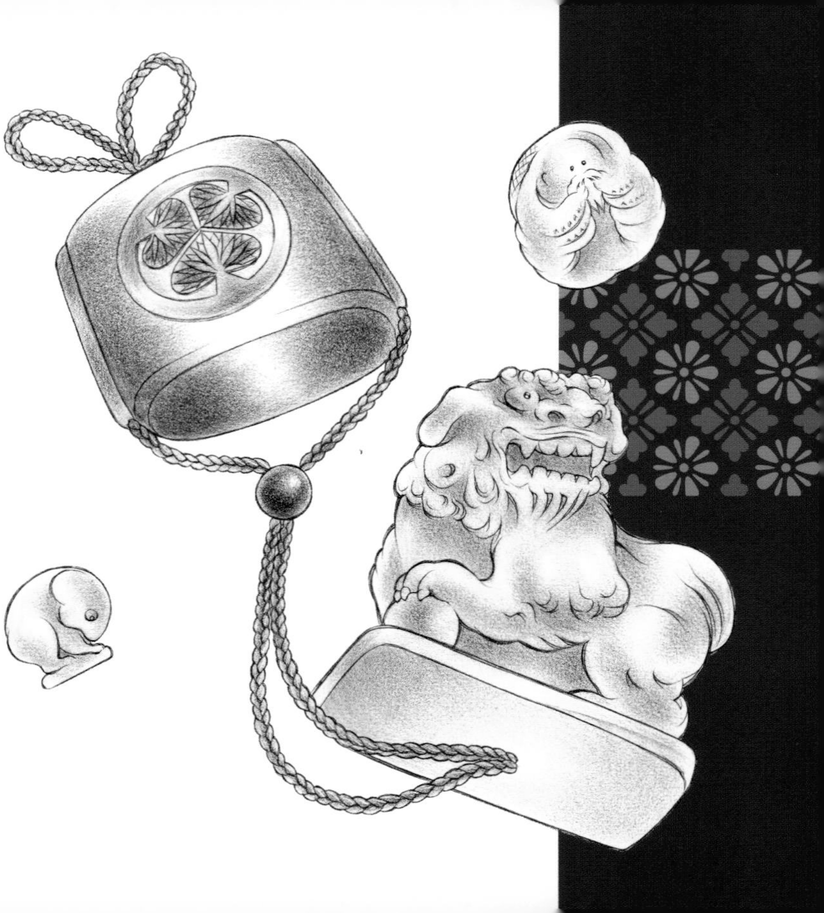

Netsuke

Tiny Treasures

Since kimono have no pockets, our Japanese ancestors carried their valuables in pouches hung from the belt. The fastener was a little carved object – the netsuke. They usually took the form of animals or deities, and were carved out of everything from wood to ivory to coral. Today, netsuke are wildly popular as collectible art.

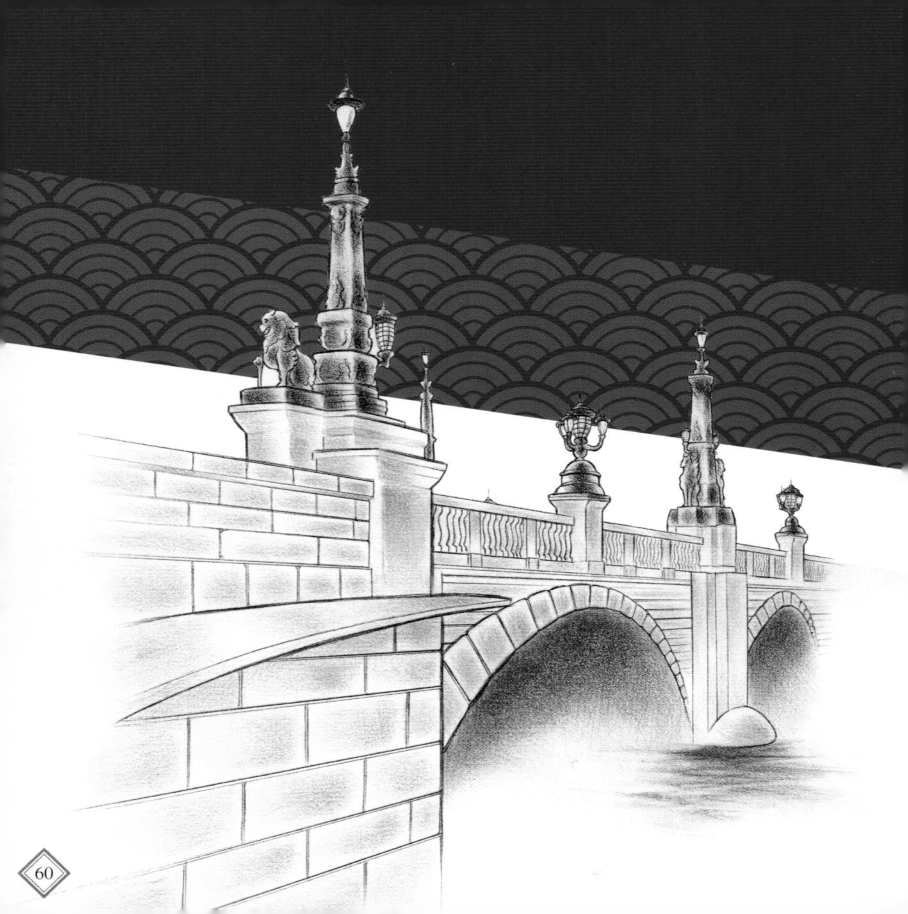

Spanning Centuries

If we see a sign that says we're 100 kilometers from Tokyo, it means more specifically that we are 100 kilometers from Nihonbashi, an elegant stone bridge in the heart of the capital. The original wooden span was a center of commerce during the Edo Period (1603-1867), and the area remains a major financial district.

日本橋

Nihonbashi

御参り

Paying Respects

A trip to a Japanese shrine involves many rituals. The most common omairi involves throwing a coin into a donation box, clapping three times, and then pausing to reflect on our visit. We may also ring a bell, or burn *senko* (incense) to cleanse our souls.

Omairi

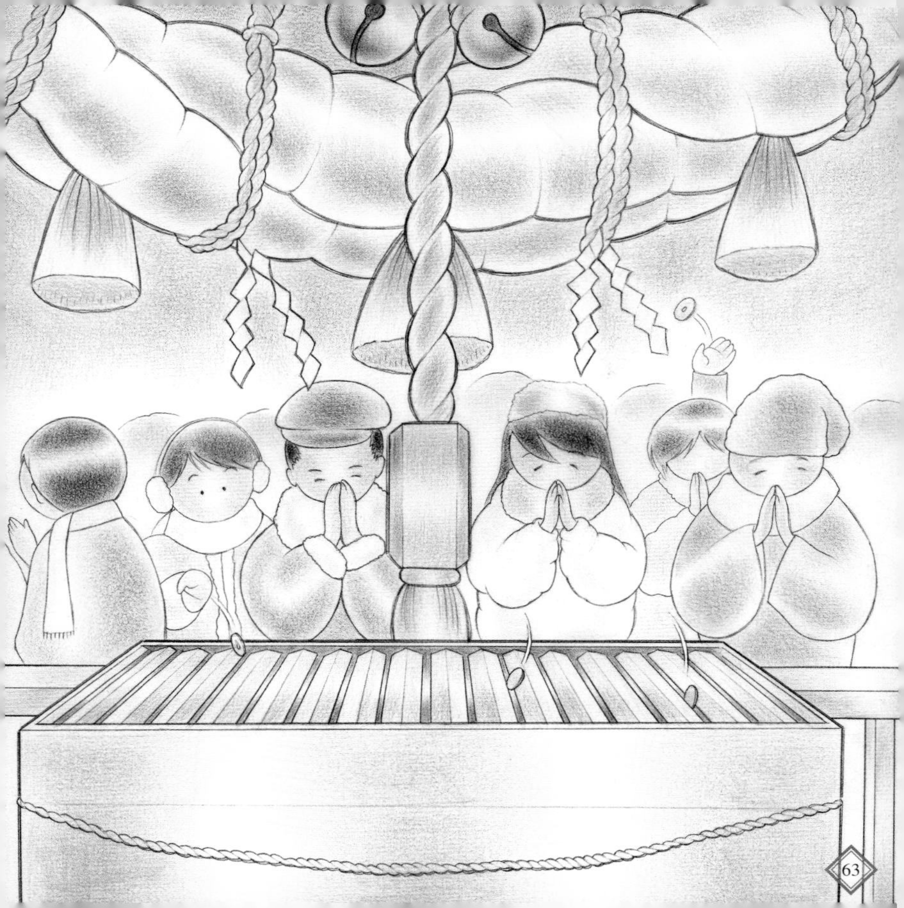

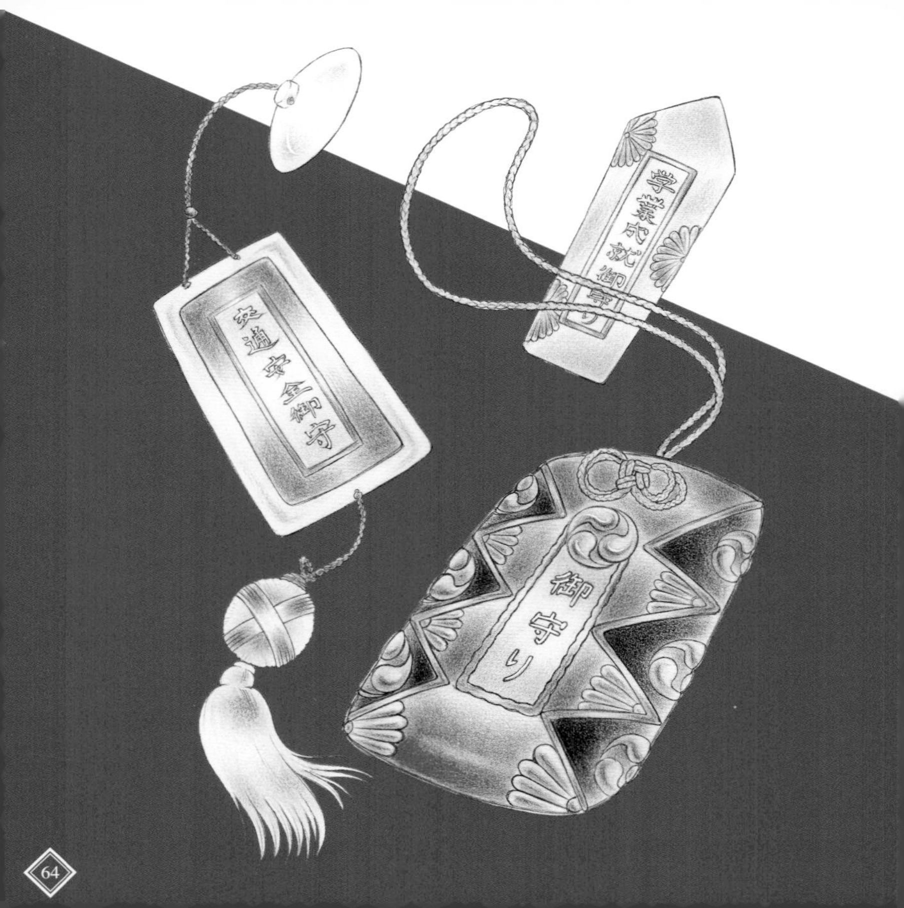
交通安全御守
学業成就御守り
御守り

Omamori
御守り

Temple Trinkets

We all need a little luck – some of us need every bit we can get! Omamori are lucky charms better than any four-leaf clover or rabbit's foot: they bring the protection of the gods. Some are very specific: there are omamori for drivers, omamori for expectant mothers and omamori for students, among others. Whatever you need help in, there's probably an omamori for you, too.

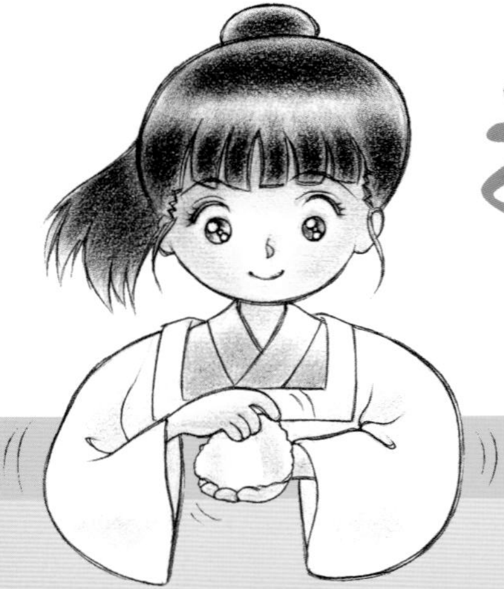

おにぎり

Super Snacks

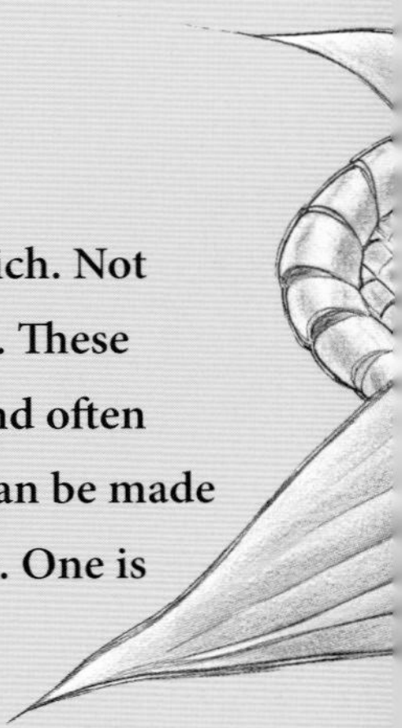

Onigiri are the Japanese equivalent of the sandwich. Not because of their ingredients, but the role they fill. These little balls of *gohan* (rice), wrapped in seaweed and often with a sour plum or piece of fish in the middle, can be made at home or bought in stores, and taken anywhere. One is a snack – two or three are a quick and easy meal.

Onigiri

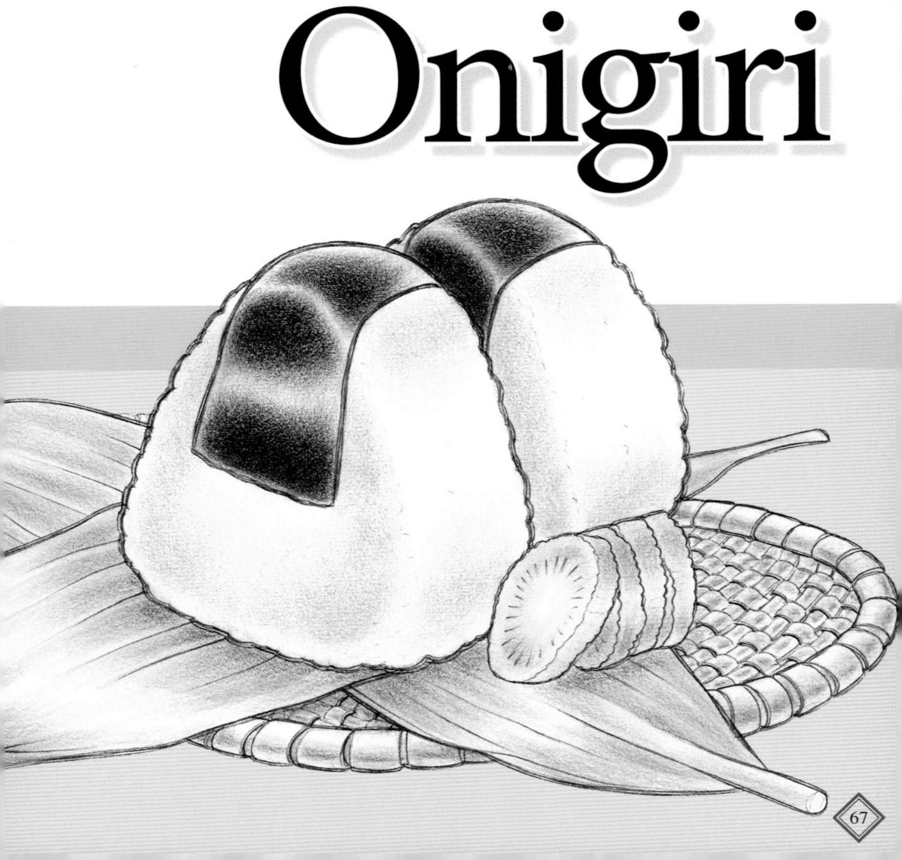

Spa Culture

No one loves a good soak as much as the Japanese. Thanks to the dozens of volcanoes scattered across the nation, thermally heated natural baths dot the landscape. Many onsen are said to have water possessed with special healing powers. Even if that's not entirely true, they sure are good for bathing!

温泉 Onsen

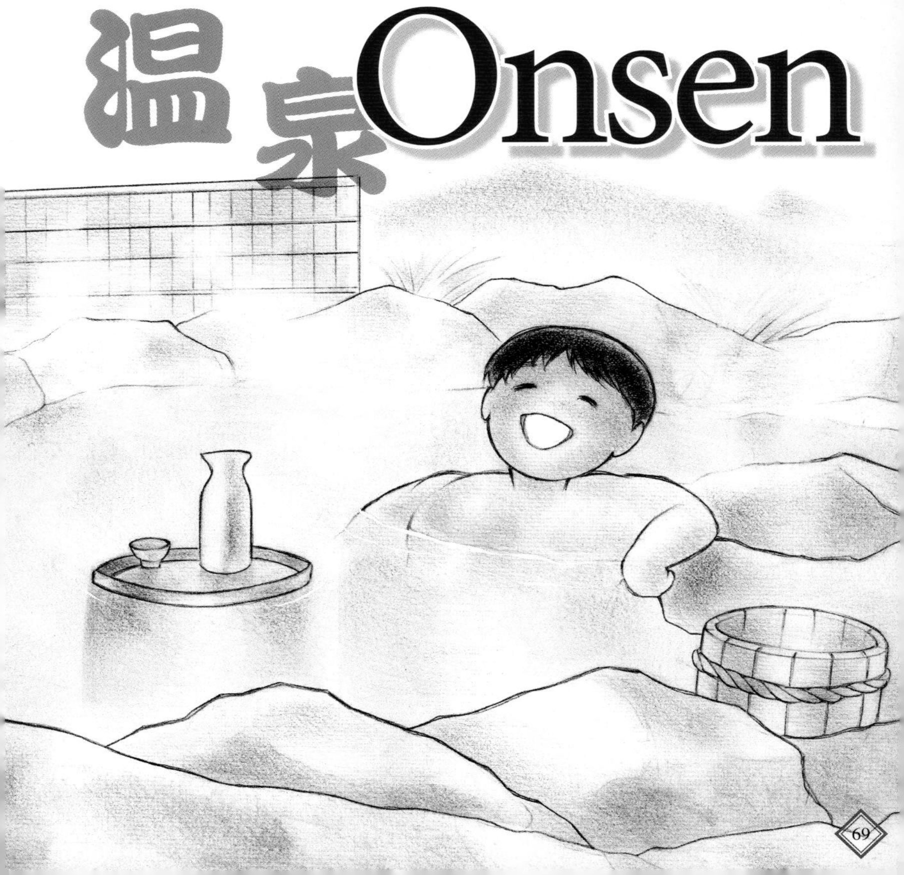

Paper Craft

折紙

Tradition dictates that if you fold a thousand paper cranes, you'll be granted one wish. Today, the paper crane is a symbol of peace, and origami remains a national passion. Why not try your own hand at this ancient art?

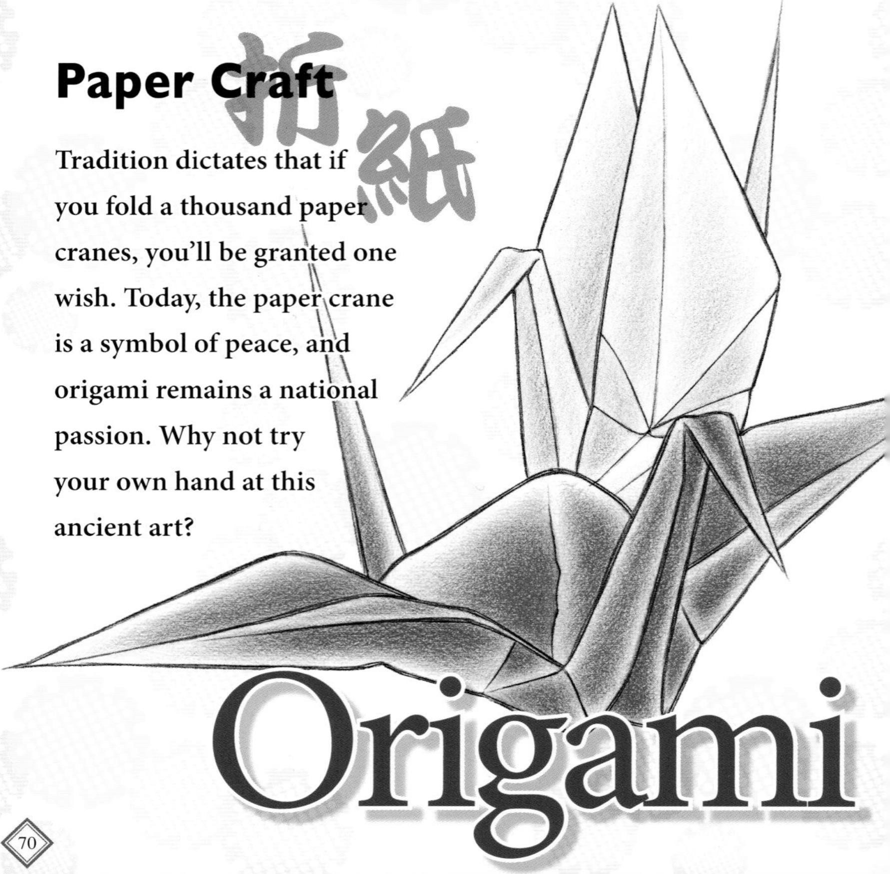

Origami

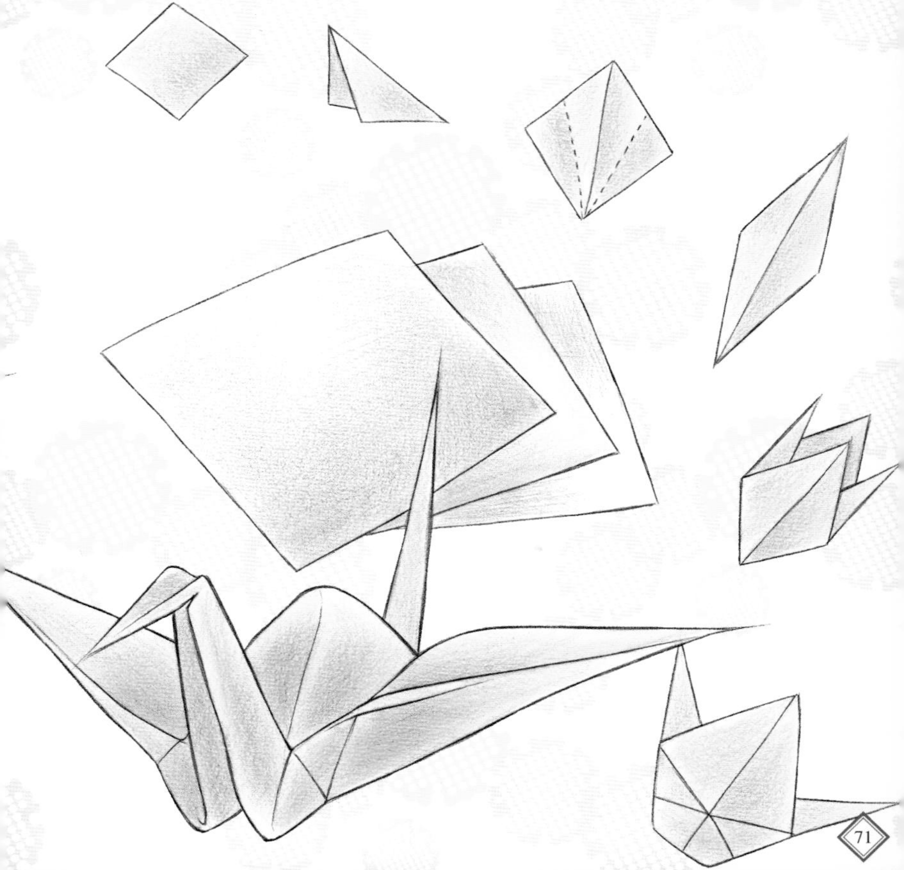

Parlor Games

A mystery to most foreigners, pachinko is a national pastime, especially among bachelors. Tourists sometimes call it "Japanese pinball," but in truth pinball and pachinko have little in common. The object of this spellbinding game of chance is to control the flow of little ball bearings so they drop through certain holes and into a tray. The more balls we collect, the more we win. Think Vegas, minus the silver dollars!

Pachinko

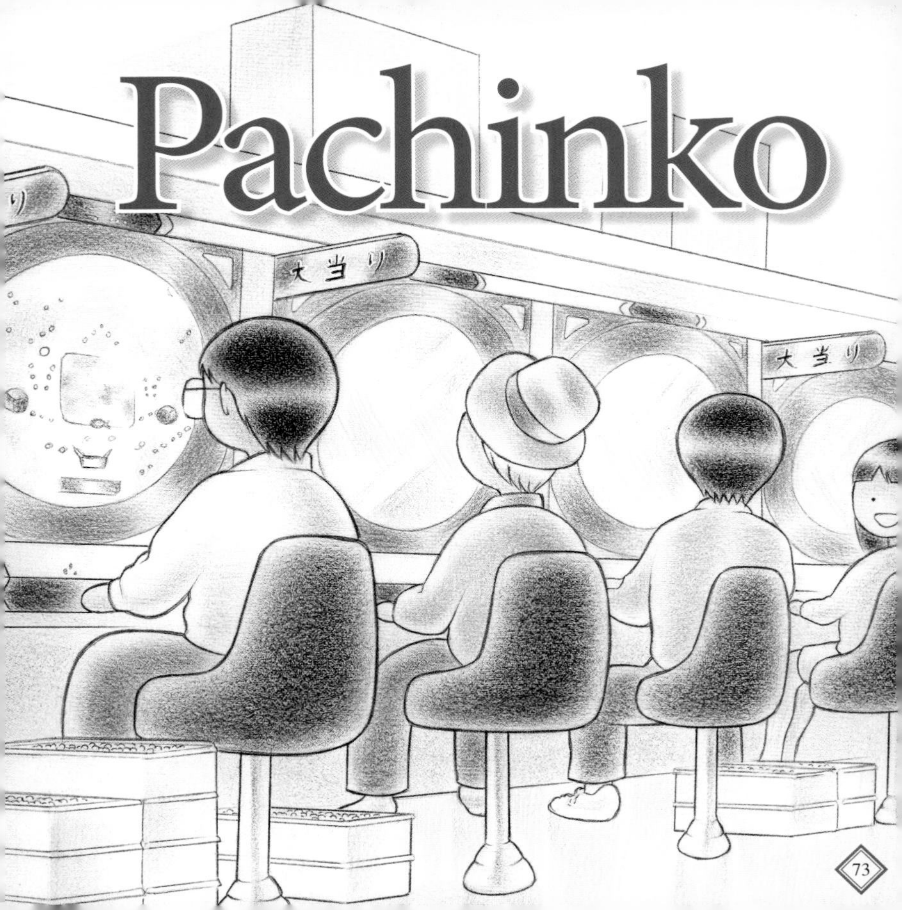
大当り
大当り

ラムネ

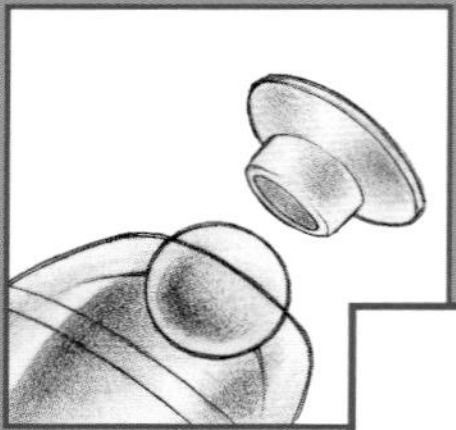

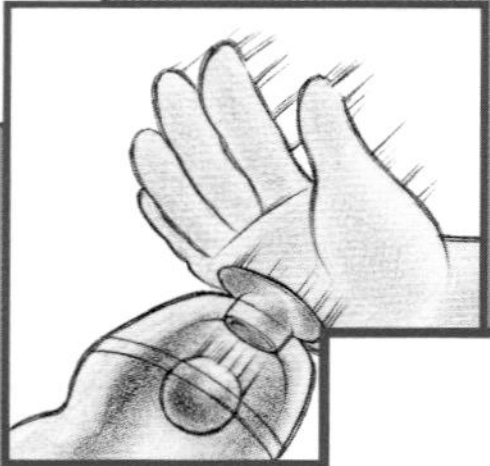

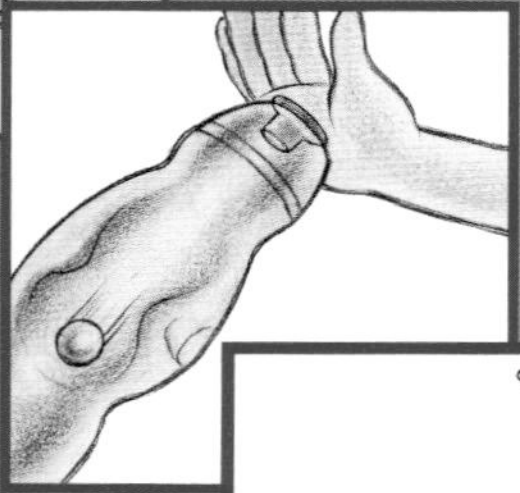

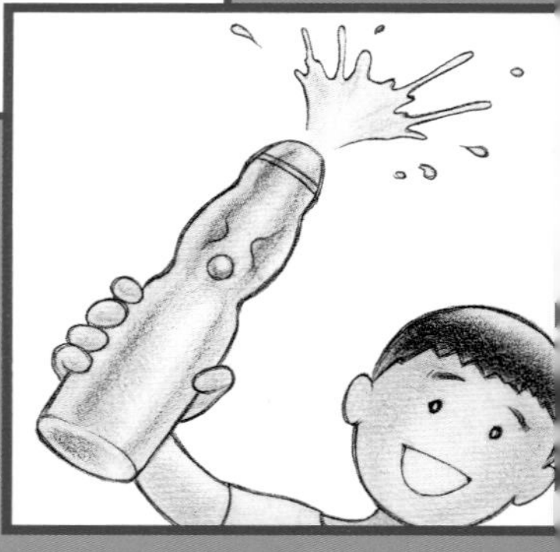

Soda "Pop"

Nothing says *natsu* (summer) like a bottle of ramune! Pull off the plastic cap, turn it over and use it to force the marble stopper into the bottle, opening the drink – often with a big sticky splash. It tastes a bit like a lemon-lime soda, but sweeter, and far more fun!

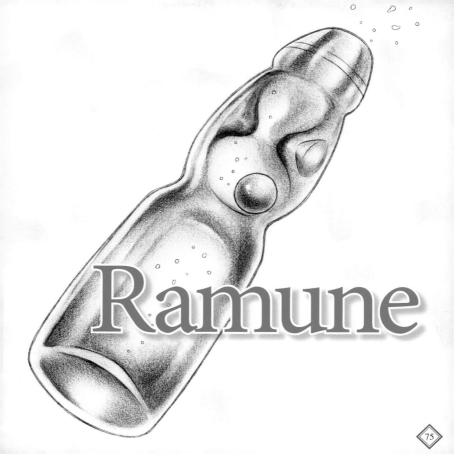

Ramune

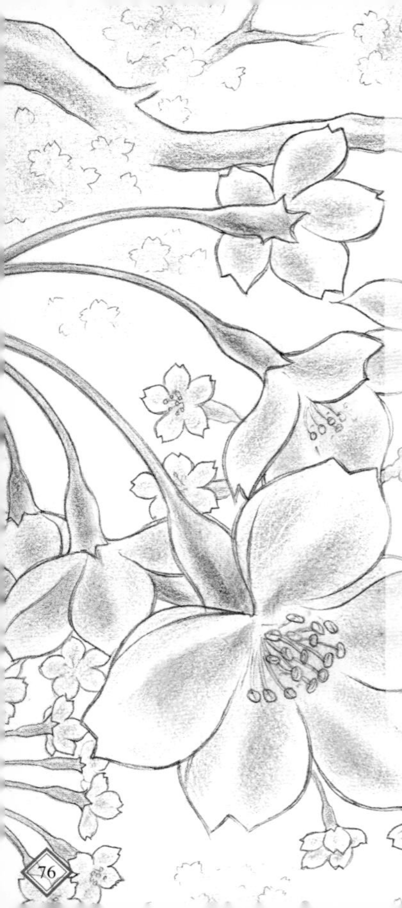

Cherry Blossoms

Just as Westerners may wait all night to score tickets to a big concert, we Japanese will wait just as long to secure the perfect spot beneath the cherry blossom trees. Here, *hanami* (flower-viewing) is a spectator sport, complete with the Japanese version of a tailgate party. The picnics held beneath the blossoms are often mighty feasts, spread out over ubiquitous blue plastic tarps, and with more than a little rice wine to go around!

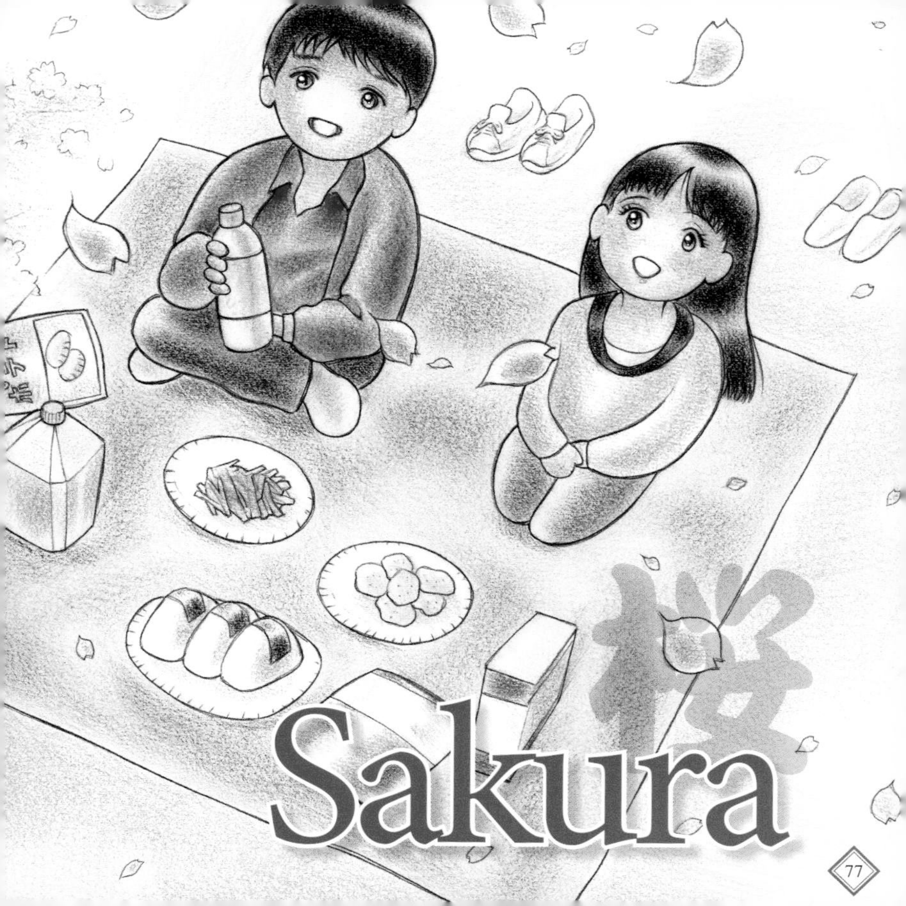
桜
Sakura

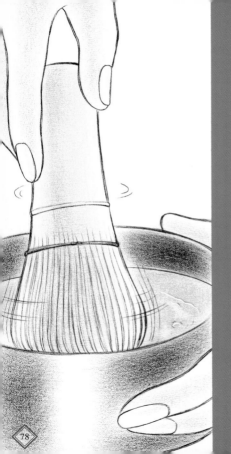

Sado

茶道

The Way of Tea

Much of Japanese culture revolves around finding deeper meaning and deriving greater pleasure from life's simplest pursuits. The tea ceremony is a spiritual affair that takes its participants far beyond the everyday act of serving and drinking *ocha* (green tea).

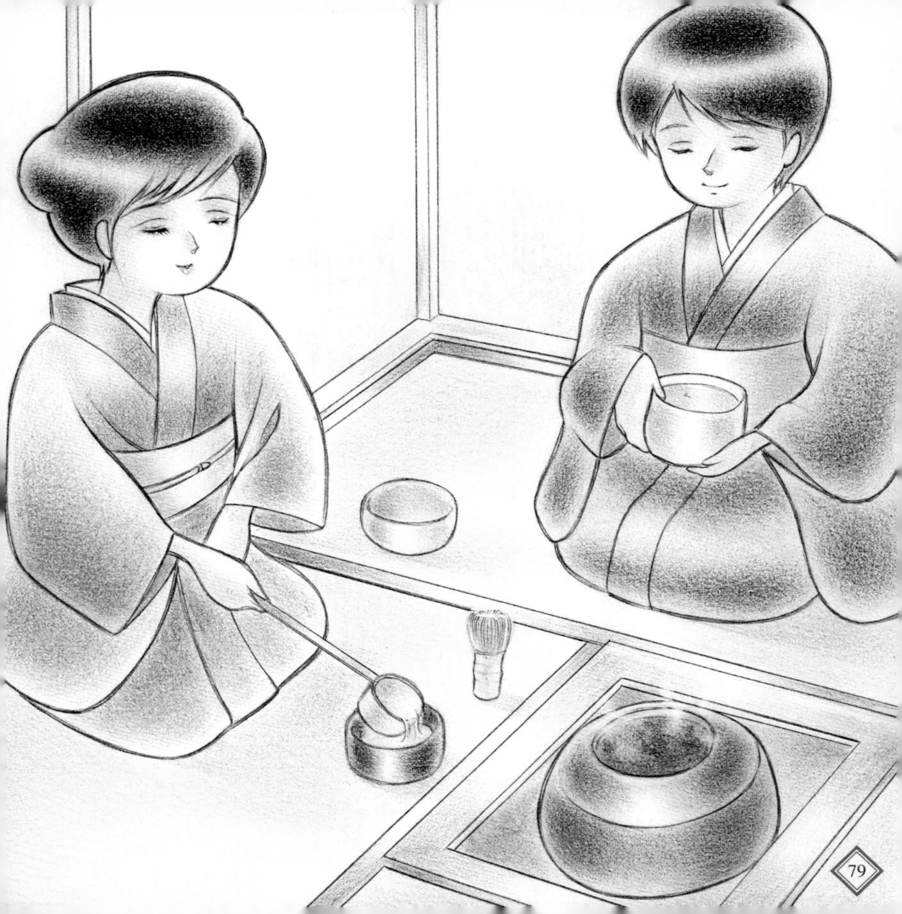

Seifuku

制服

Style Points

In Japan, we like to dress for success. Our most famous uniform is the sailor suit worn by schoolgirls. In fact, that's where the word seifuku comes from, combining *sei* (for sailor) with *fuku* (clothes). But it really refers to any kind of uniform, up to and including the outfits worn by office workers.

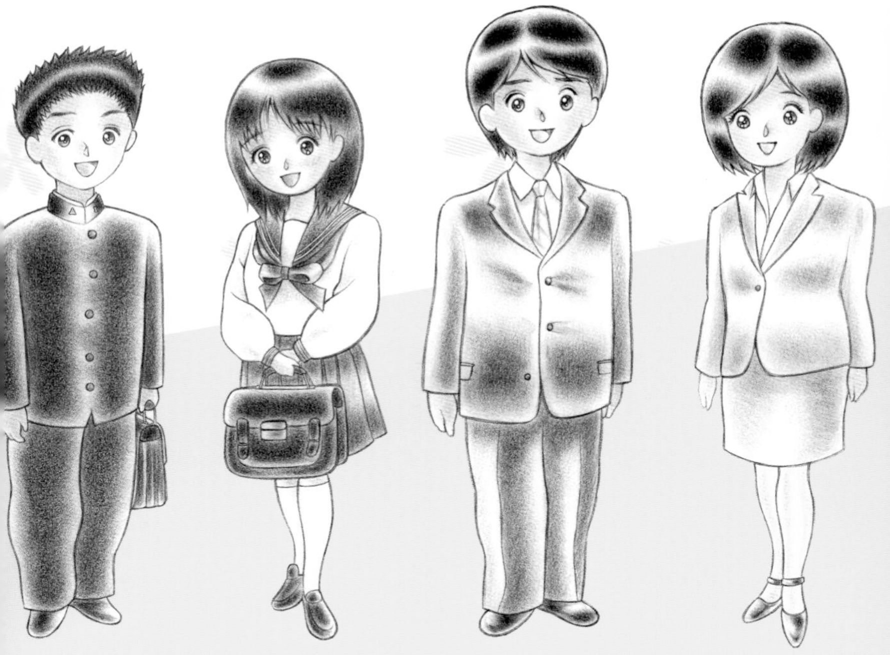

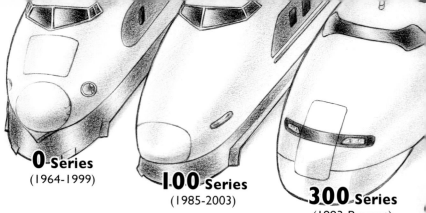

0-Series
(1964-1999)

100-Series
(1985-2003)

300-Series
(1993-Present)

Bullet Trains

新幹線

We can get anywhere in Japan by train, but nothing beats the speed of the Shinkansen – the renowned "bullet trains." These are the world's fastest regularly scheduled passenger trains, and have been running right on schedule since the mid-1960s. For a real thrill, sit in the dining car and watch the speedometer top 300 kph!

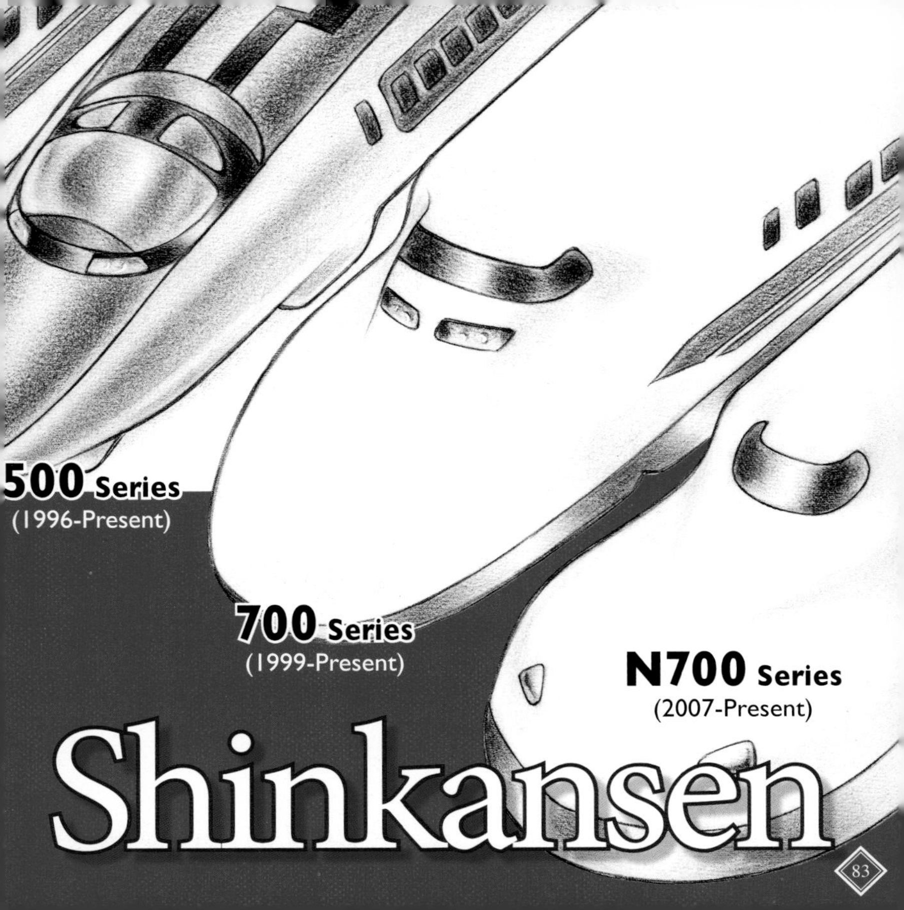
500 Series
(1996-Present)
700 Series
(1999-Present)
N700 Series
(2007-Present)
Shinkansen

Samurai Strongholds

Japanese castles, like their European counterparts, were the bastions of warlords and feudal families, and remain popular as tourist attractions today. But the original structures were made largely of wood, so many burned down and were rebuilt several times over. In fact, Osaka Castle, pictured here, is a modern concrete structure complete with an elevator!

Shiro

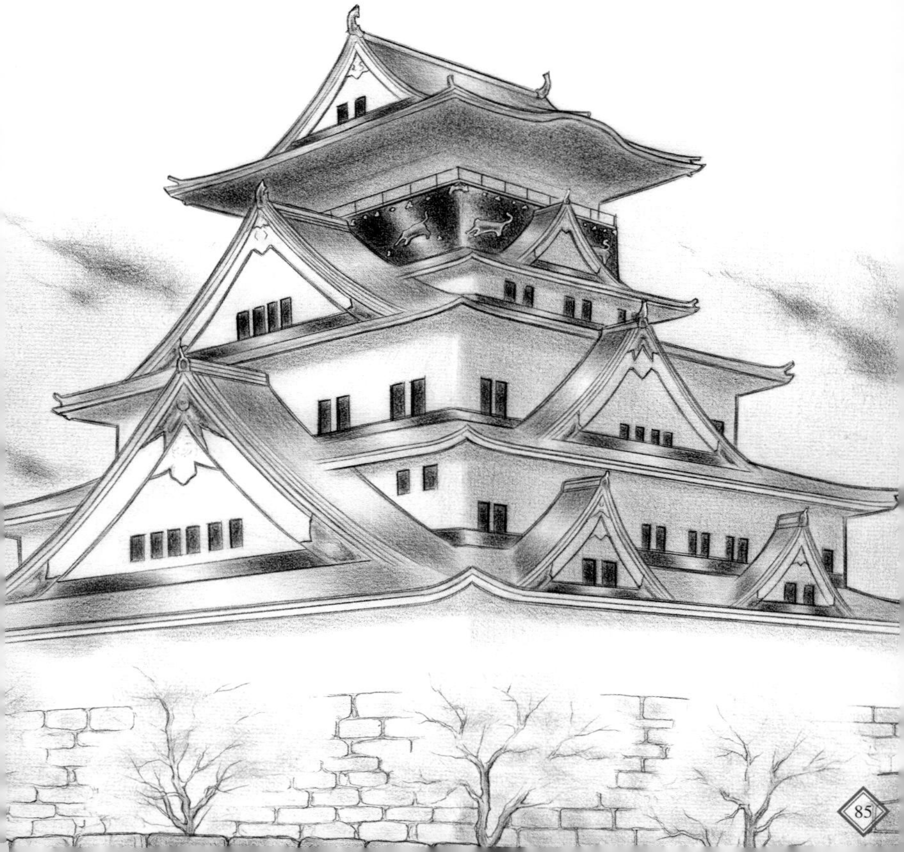

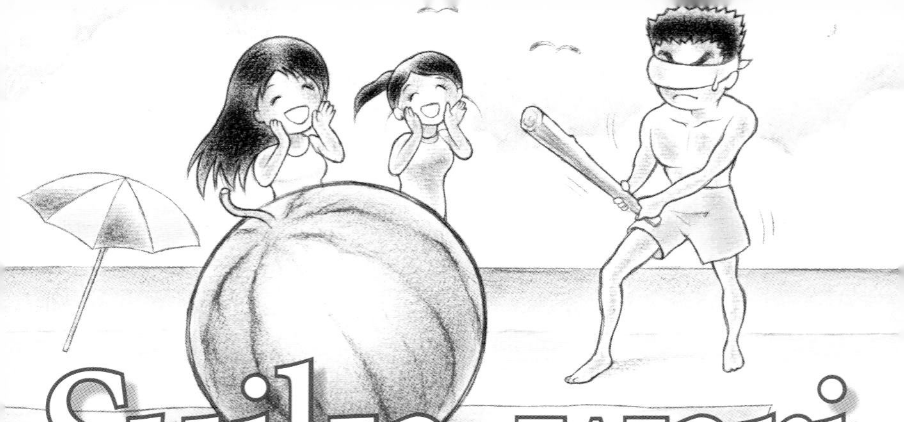

Suika-wari

Smashing Fun 西瓜割り

A *suika* (watermelon) isn't just a delicious fruit: it's also the centerpiece of a great summer game. A player is blindfolded, spun around, and given a stick. The goal: smash the melon so it can be eaten! It's usually – but not always – played at the beach.

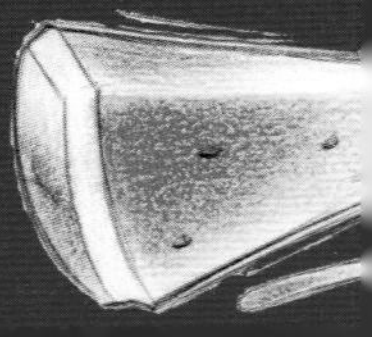

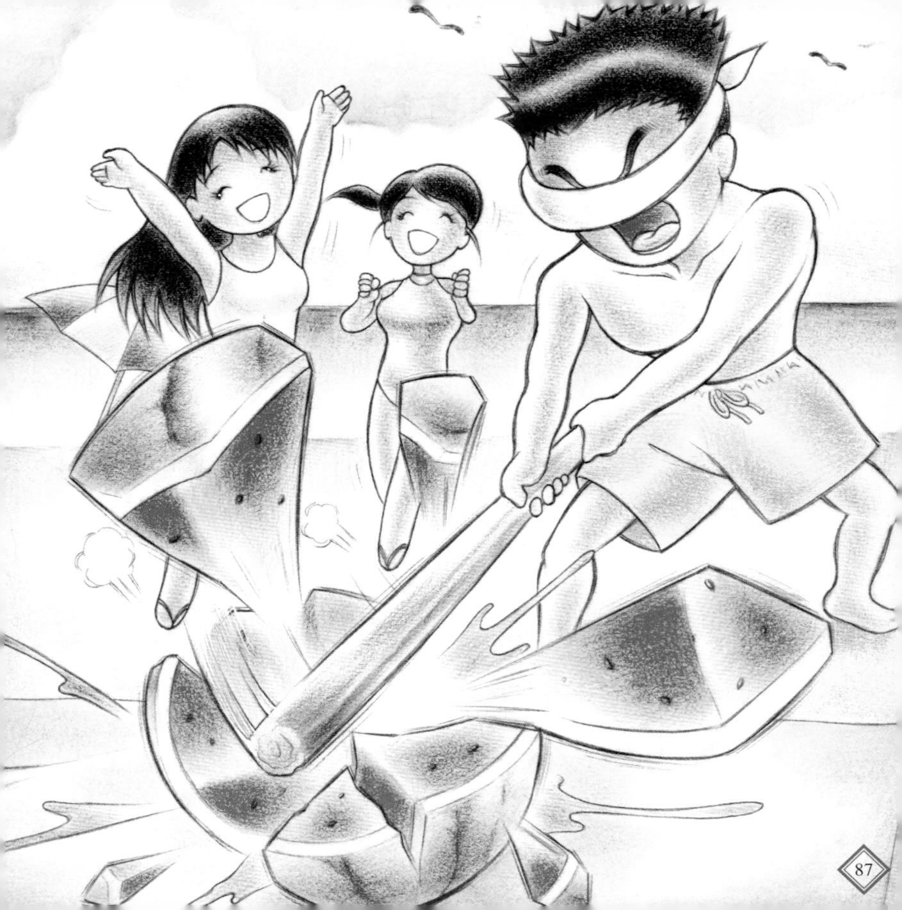

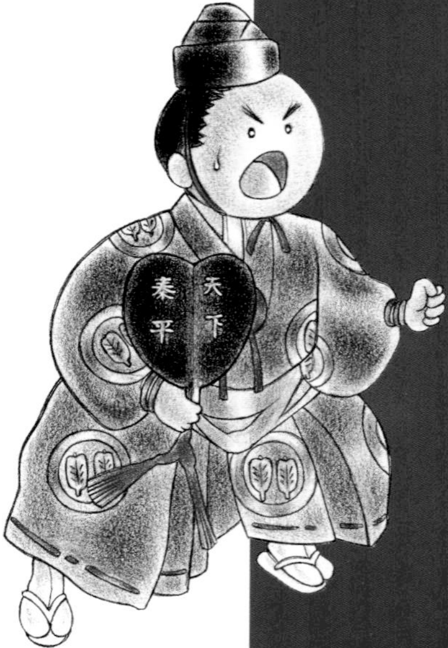
天下
泰平

Heavy Hitters

The paradox of Japan in sport: what looks like one thing on the surface is in fact something completely different. To Western eyes, two fat men shoving each other around. But look more closely: despite their weight, these are highly agile world-class athletes. The silk-robed *gyoji* (referee) shouts instructions to the wrestlers as they do battle.

Sumo

撲

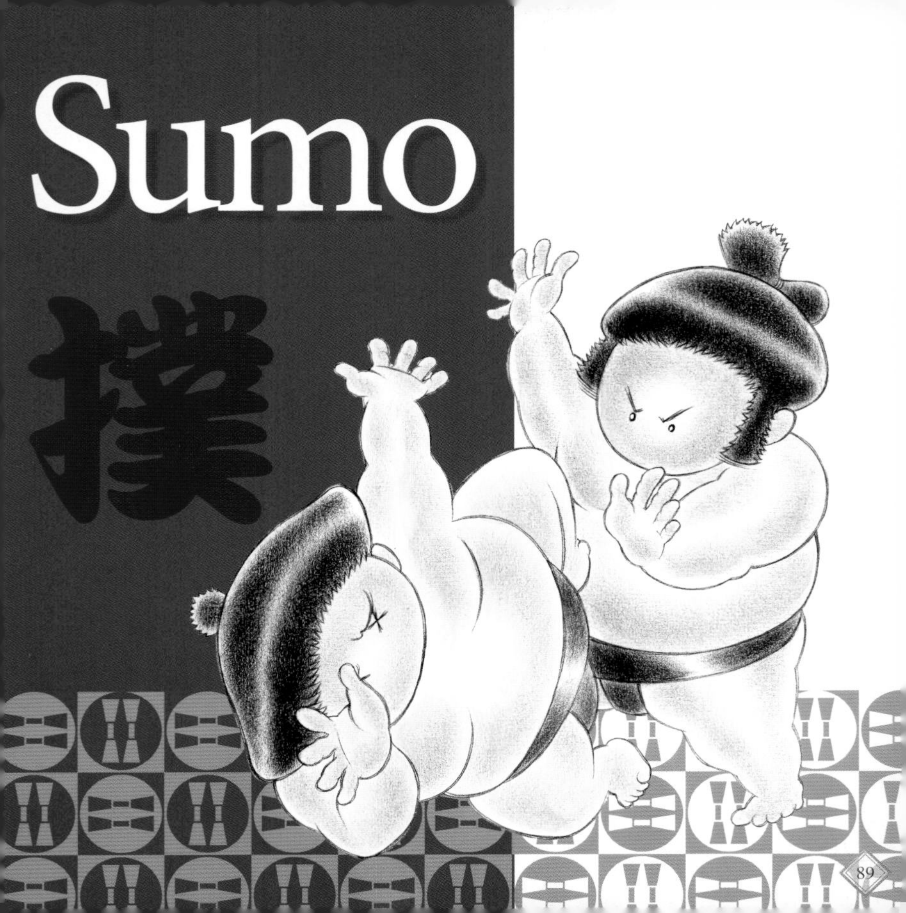

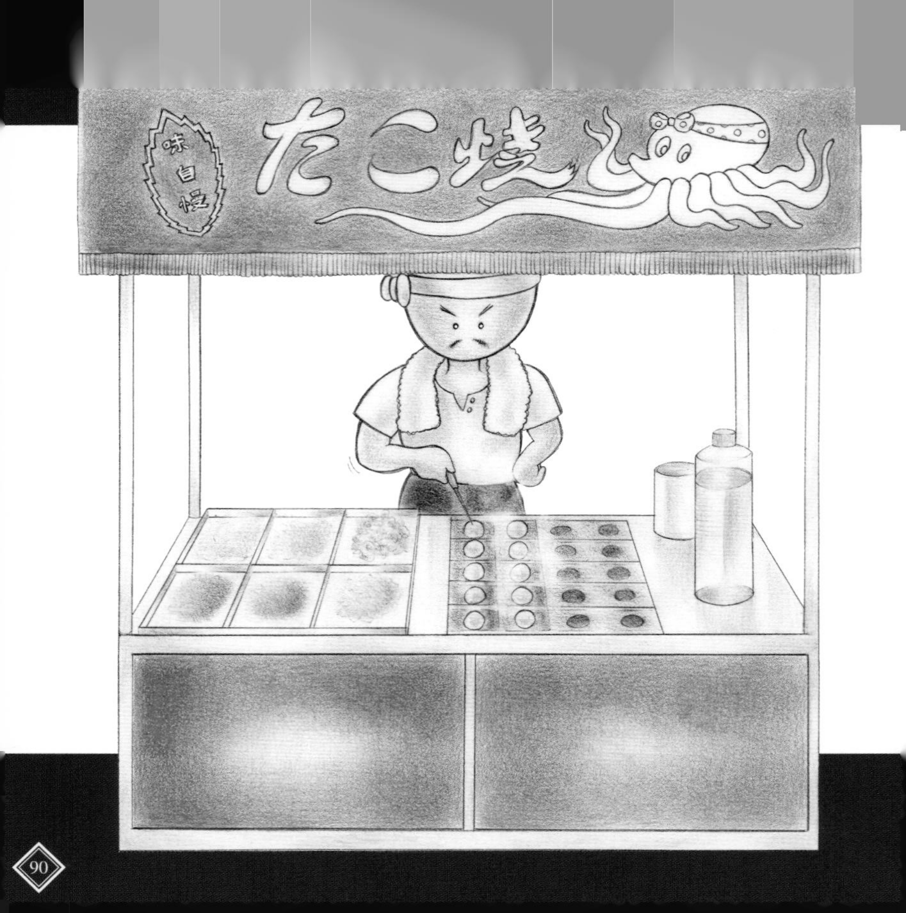
味自慢
たこ焼き

Takoyaki たこ焼き

Deep-Sea Dumplings

They look like little meatballs, and are a favorite fast food in Japan. It's octopus inside a dumpling! Takoyaki vendors often set up stalls on the sidewalk on cool autumn nights, a little treat for the walk home after a long day at work.

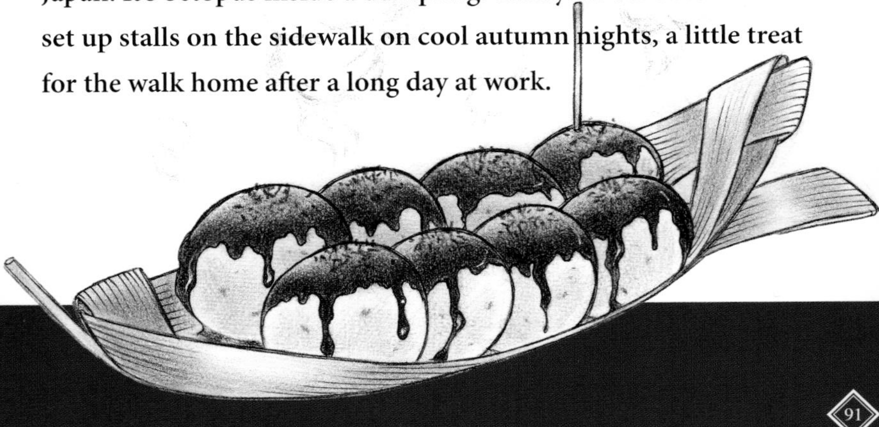

Tango no sekku

Flying Fish

Japan honors its youngest generation with national holiday called *kodomo no hi*, or Children's Day. Part of the celebration is tango no sekku, the boys' festival. Families with young sons display *kabuto* (military helmets), and around the nation, *koinobori* (carp-shaped windsocks) can be seen flapping in the spring breeze.

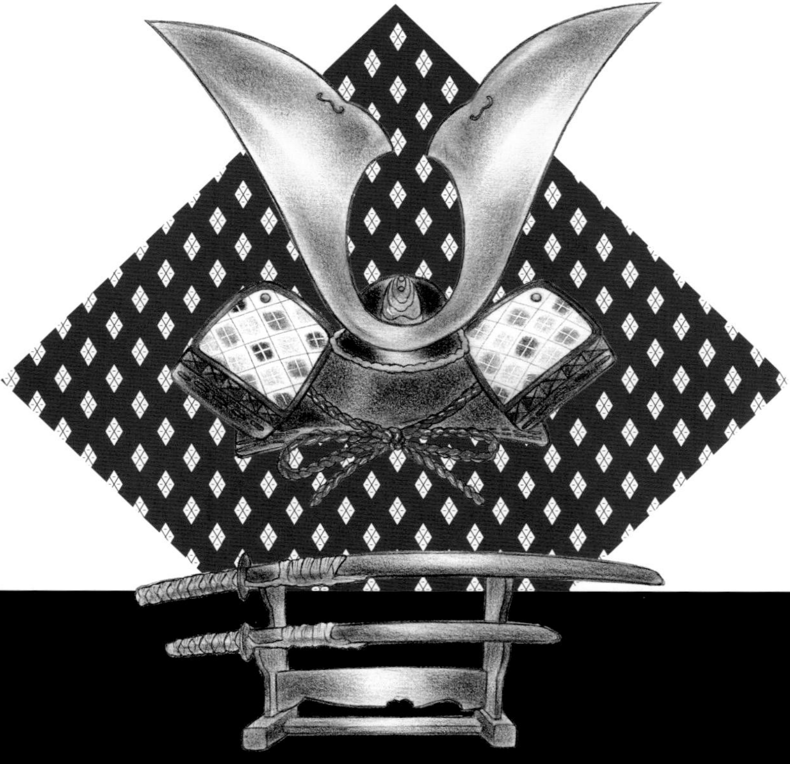

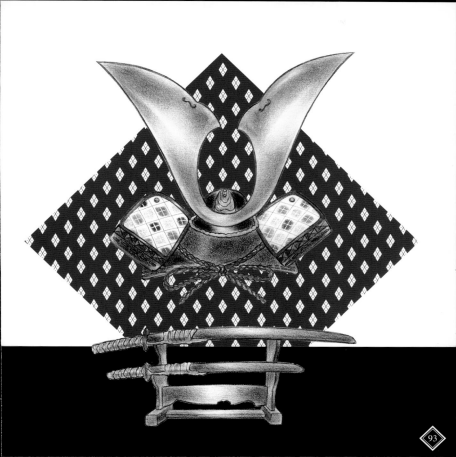

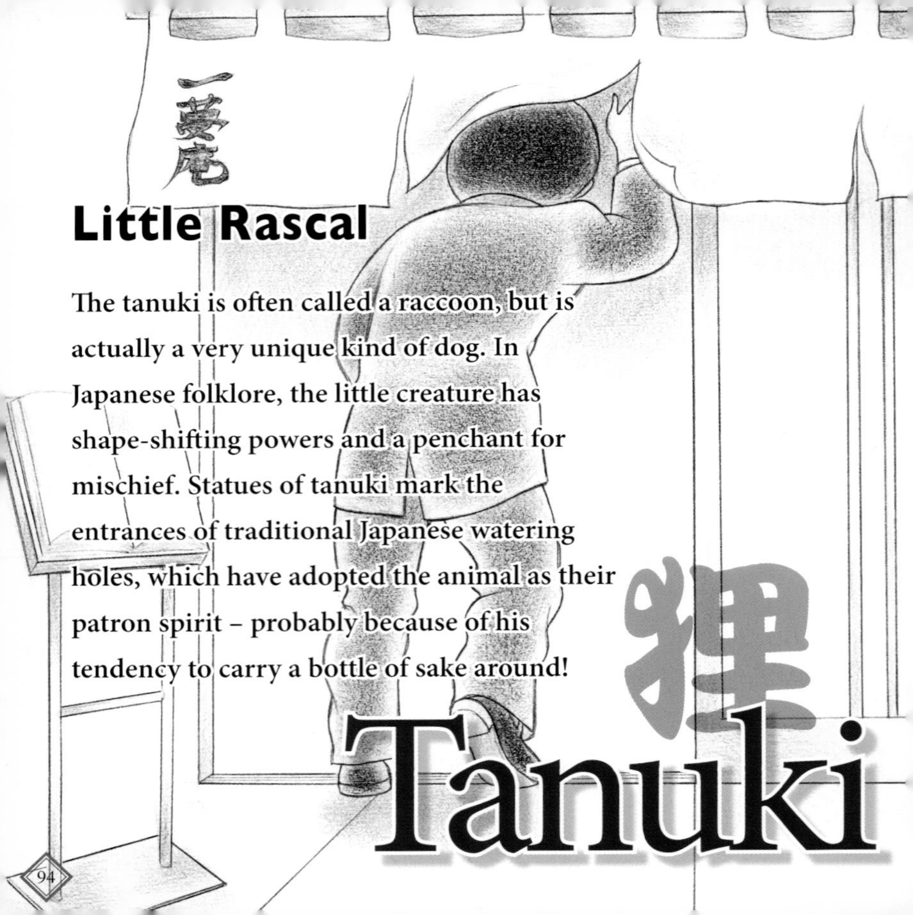

Little Rascal

The tanuki is often called a raccoon, but is actually a very unique kind of dog. In Japanese folklore, the little creature has shape-shifting powers and a penchant for mischief. Statues of tanuki mark the entrances of traditional Japanese watering holes, which have adopted the animal as their patron spirit – probably because of his tendency to carry a bottle of sake around!

狸 Tanuki

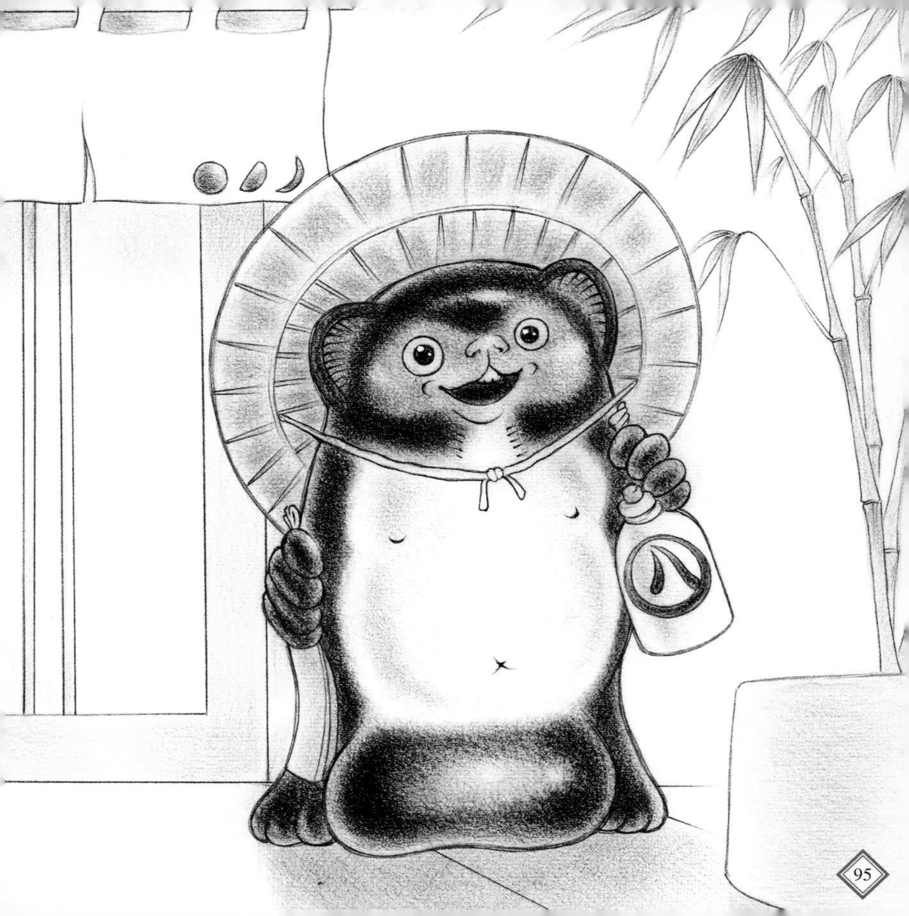

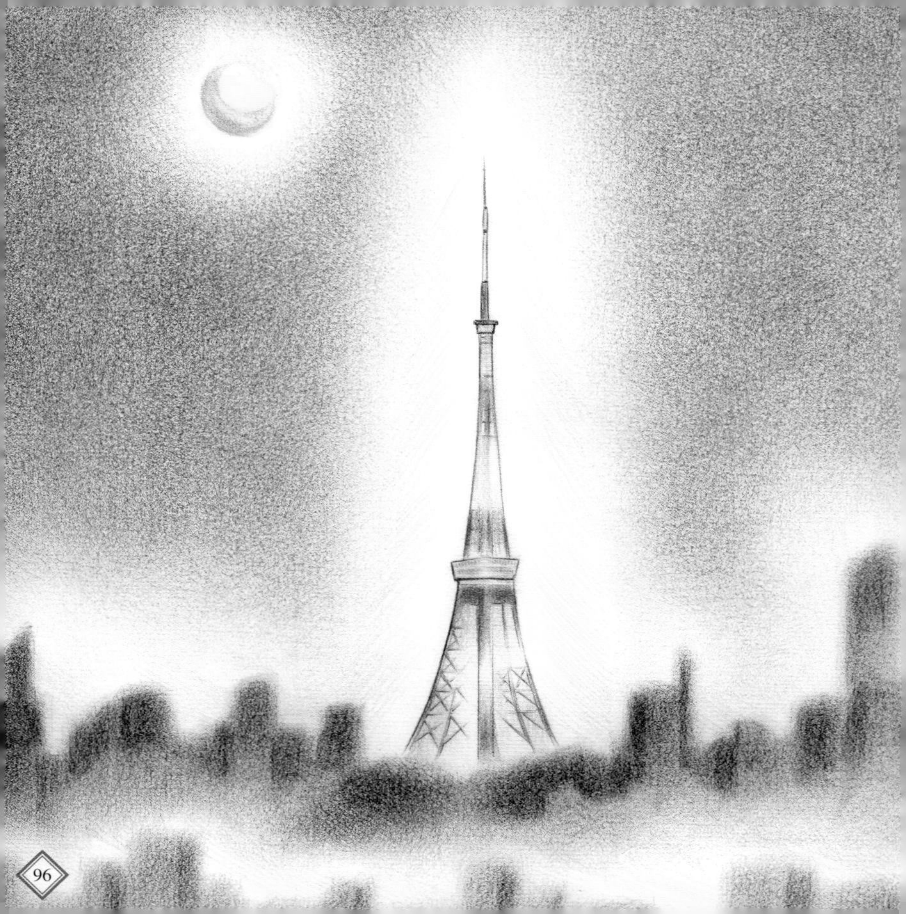

Tokyo Tower

東京タワー

Eiffel of the East

We'll always have Paris – and if you can't make it there, we'll always have Tokyo, too. Based on the Eiffel Tower, Tokyo's landmark is actually taller (1091 feet versus 1063 feet). And like its French cousin, the orange-and-white tower is a regular highlight of tourism videos, a place young couples kiss atop, and a design that has inspired countless die-cast souvenirs!

Sacred Gates

Pass beneath the torii and you undergo a symbolic journey from one world to another: the physical to the spiritual. Torii gates often lead to Shinto shrines, but can also be found at Buddhist temples. According to legend, the gates were used to help lure the sun goddess out of her cave.

Torii

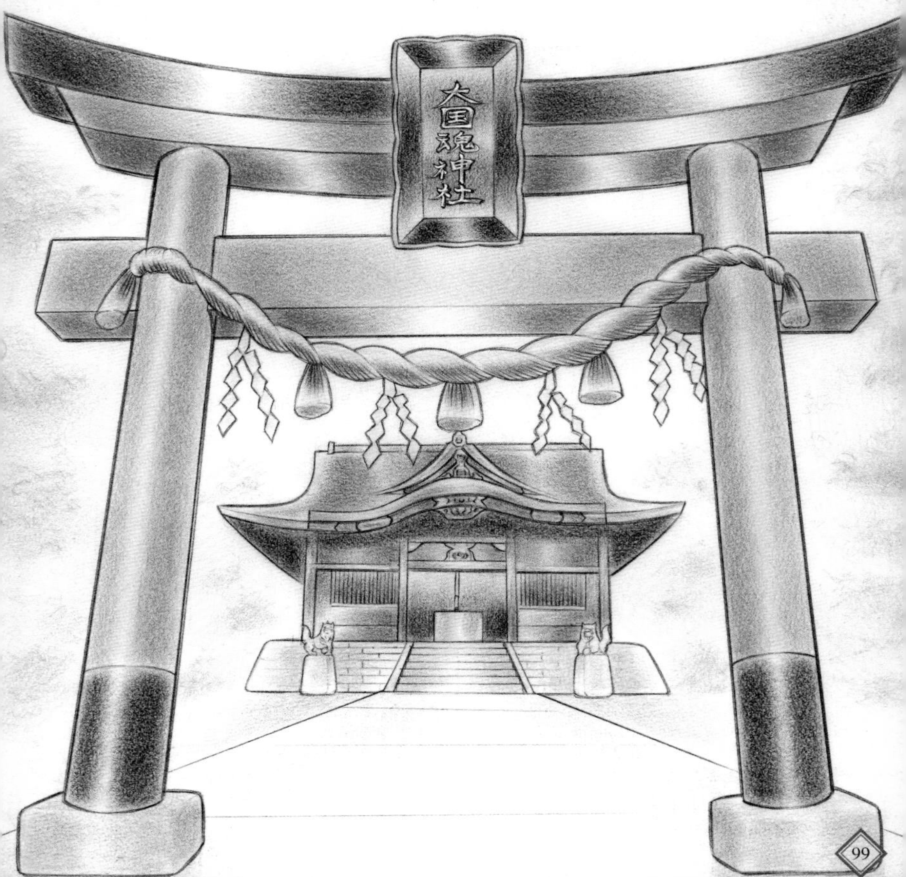
大国魂神社

Tsukiji
築地

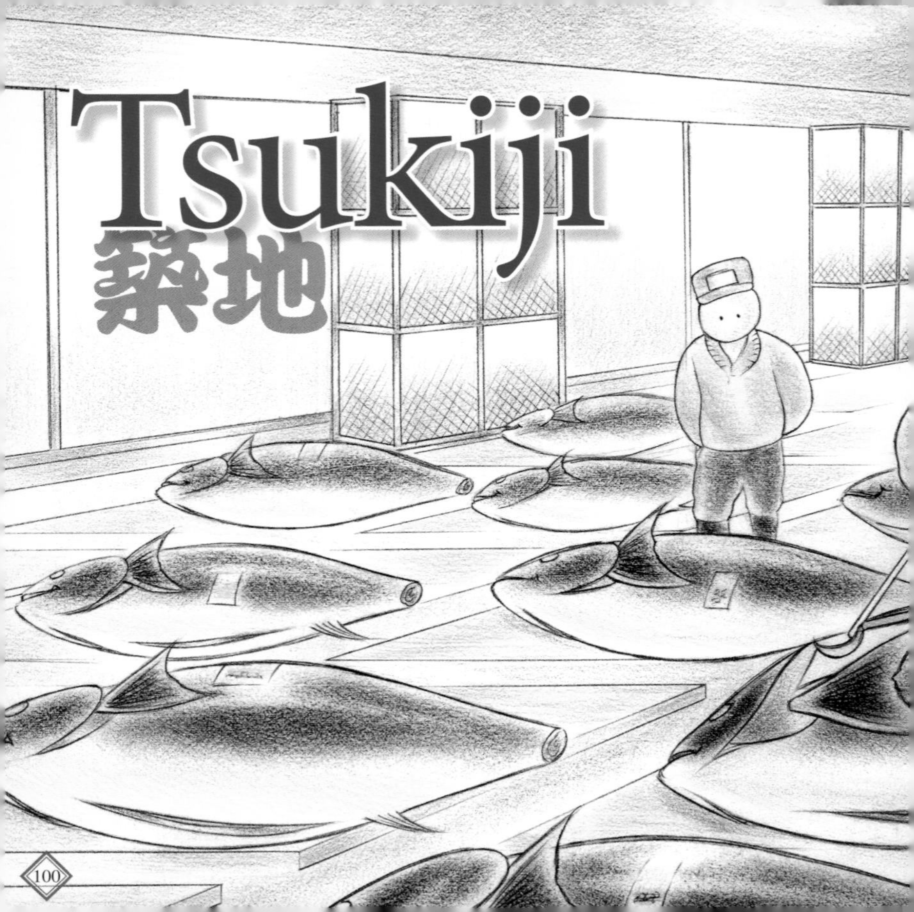

Catch of the Day

Fish as far as the eye can see! The energy and – quite literally – the flavor of Tokyo, all in one place. Tsukiji is the world's largest fish market – and in fact one of the world's largest markets of any kind. If you're visiting, get there just before dawn, when the catch comes in and goes right to the auction block.

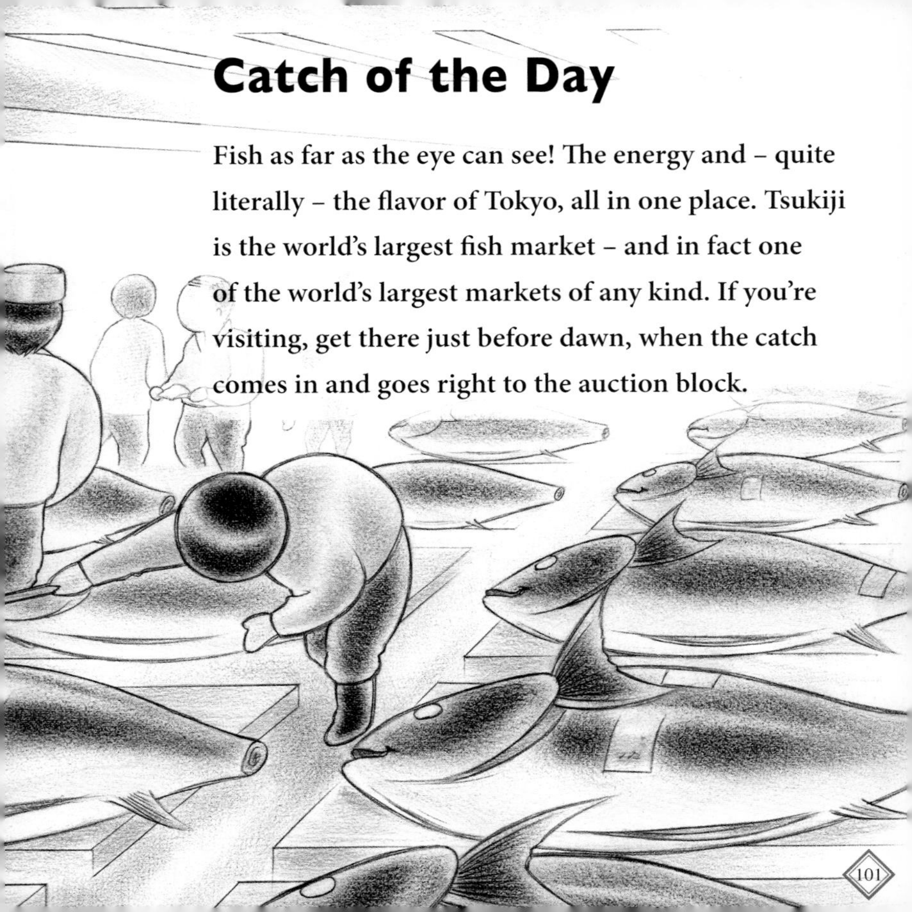

Sports Day

Every school has one: a day each year where the learning stops and the games begin. There's usually a red team and a white team, and they compete in everything from tug-of-war and dancing to a few games – such as mooncake-eating contests – you won't see anywhere else!

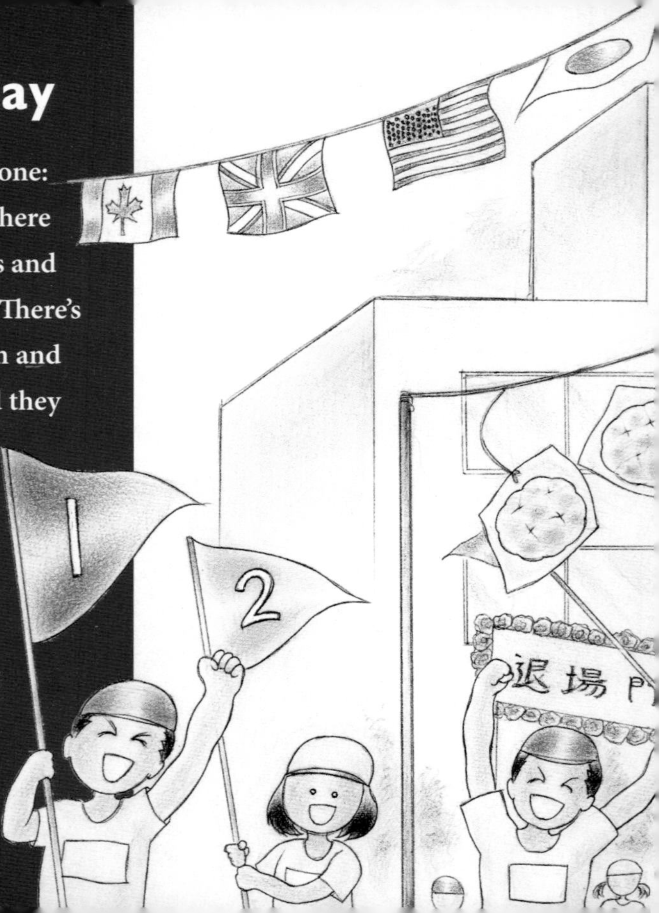

1
2
退場

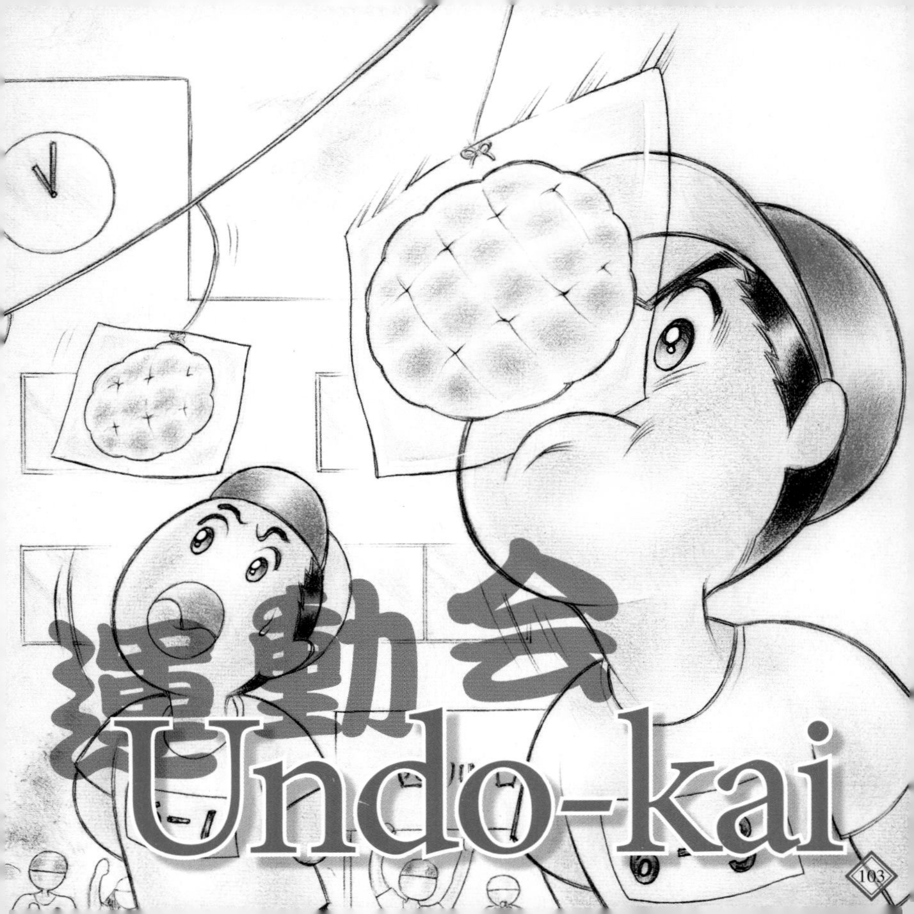

運動会 Undo-kai

Tater Trucks

In the West, you have ice cream trucks. In Japan, we can buy just about everything else off a truck. The most famous of these mobile vendors is the yakiimo man, who drives around singing about his delicious cargo: baked sweet potatoes. Many are legendary for their gravelly singing voices – and smooth taste of their potatoes.

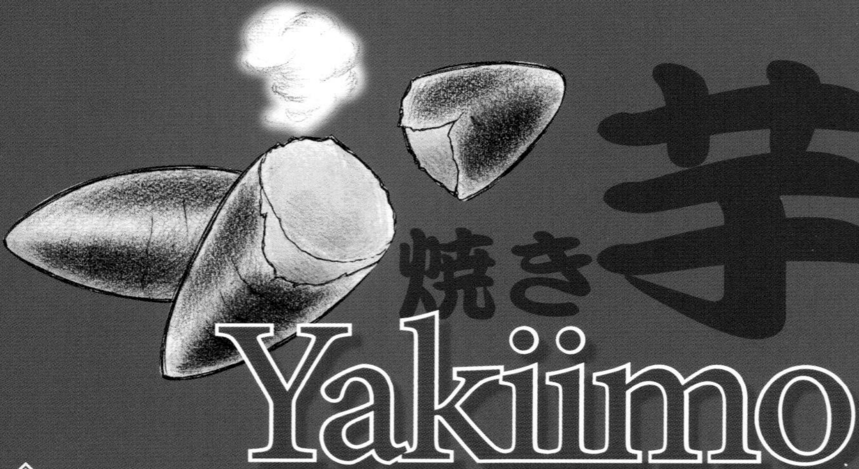
焼き芋
Yakiimo

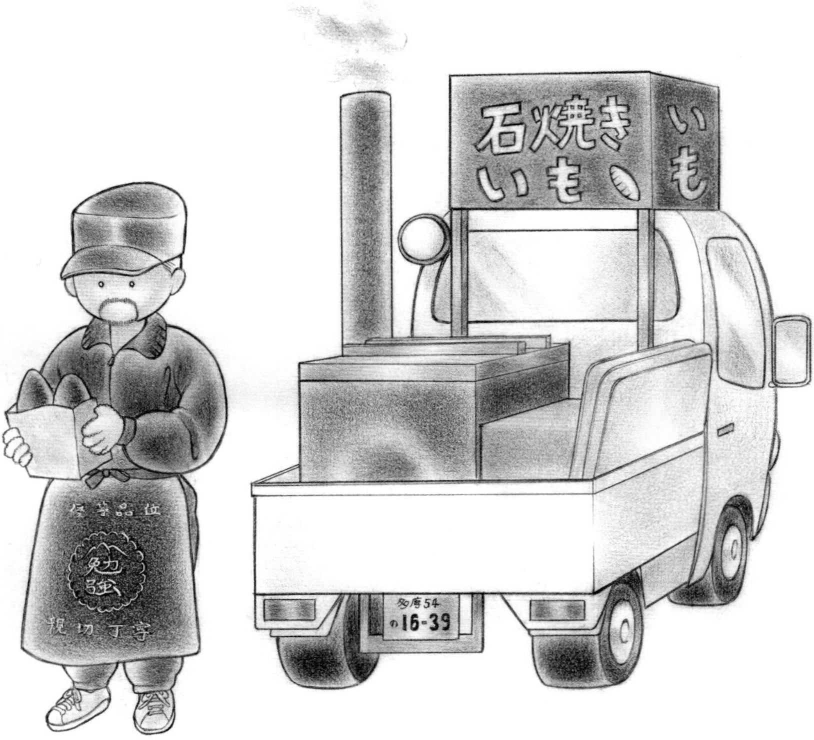
石焼き
いも
いも
優等品位
勉強
親切丁寧
の16-39

Chicken Delight

焼き鳥

It literally means flame-broiled chicken, but you can get just about anything grilled up and served on a stick at your favorite yakitori stand, along with some great big mugs of beer – and plenty of gossip. Be sure to try the *tsukune* – chicken meatballs.

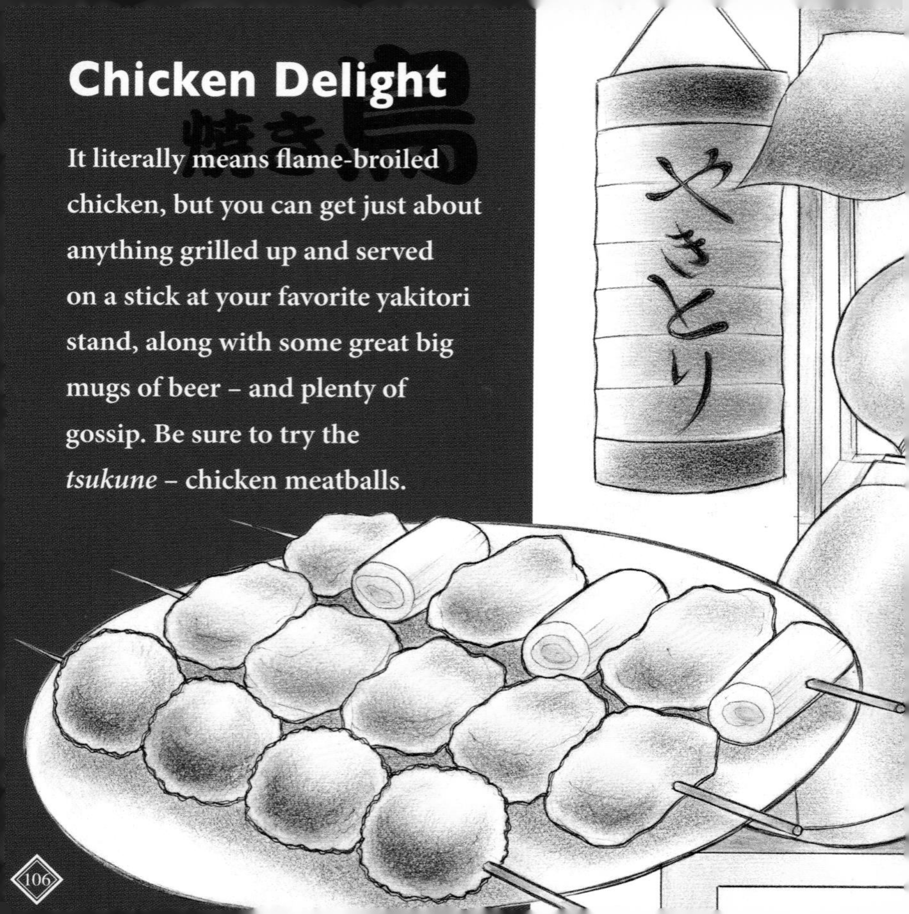
やきとり

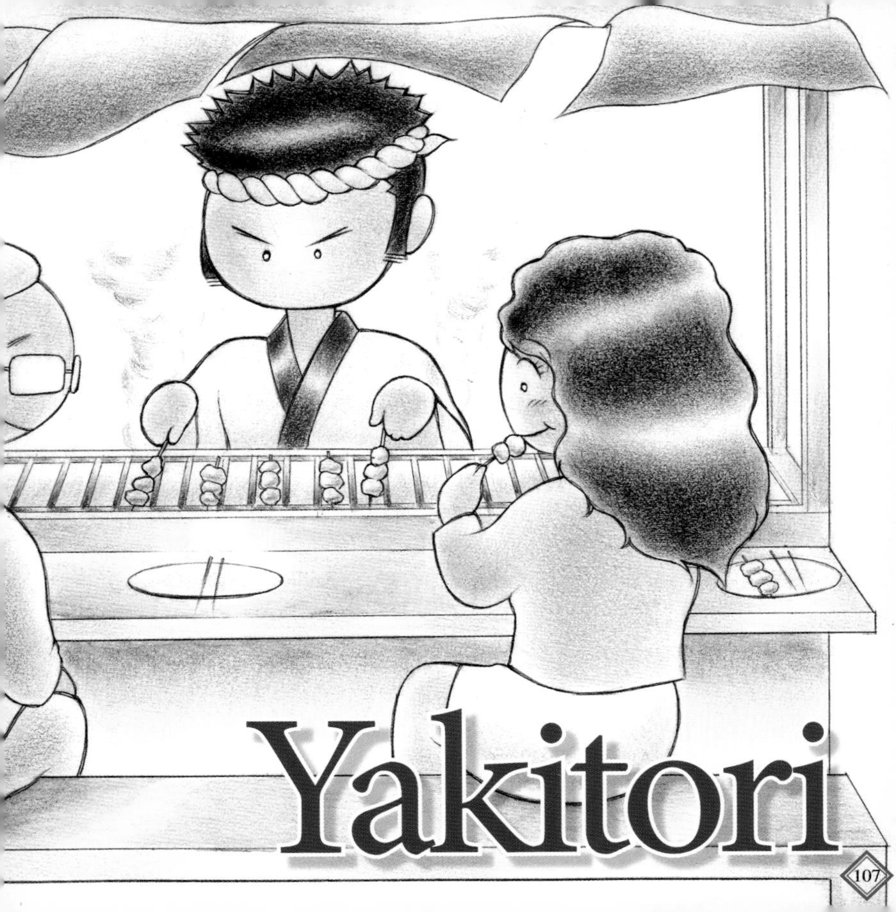

Yakitori

Way of Life

The spirit of a washitsu (literally "Japanese room") is more than just the straw tatami mats on the floor. There is an alcove for a small shrine or art. The sliding doors are made of delicate rice paper. And the only furniture in the room is usually a low table, where everything from eating to studying to resting a weary head is done. Welcome to Japan!

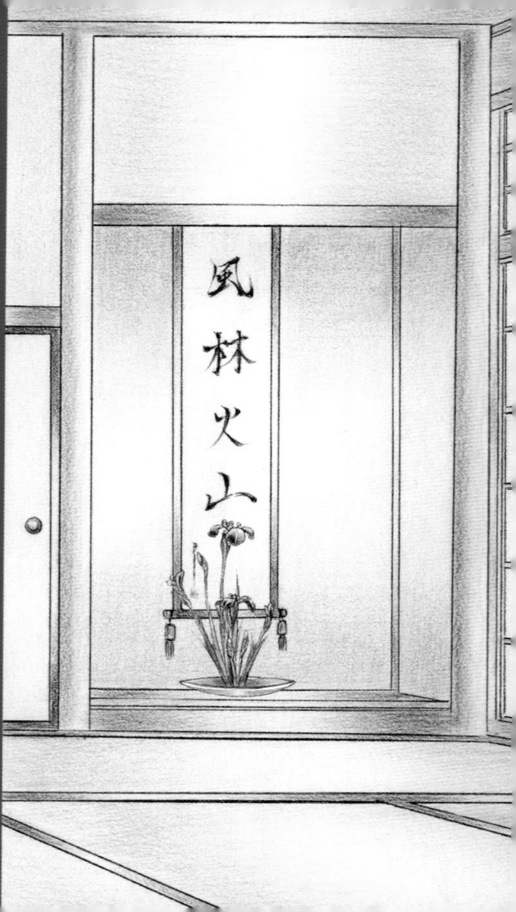
風林火山

和室 Washitsu

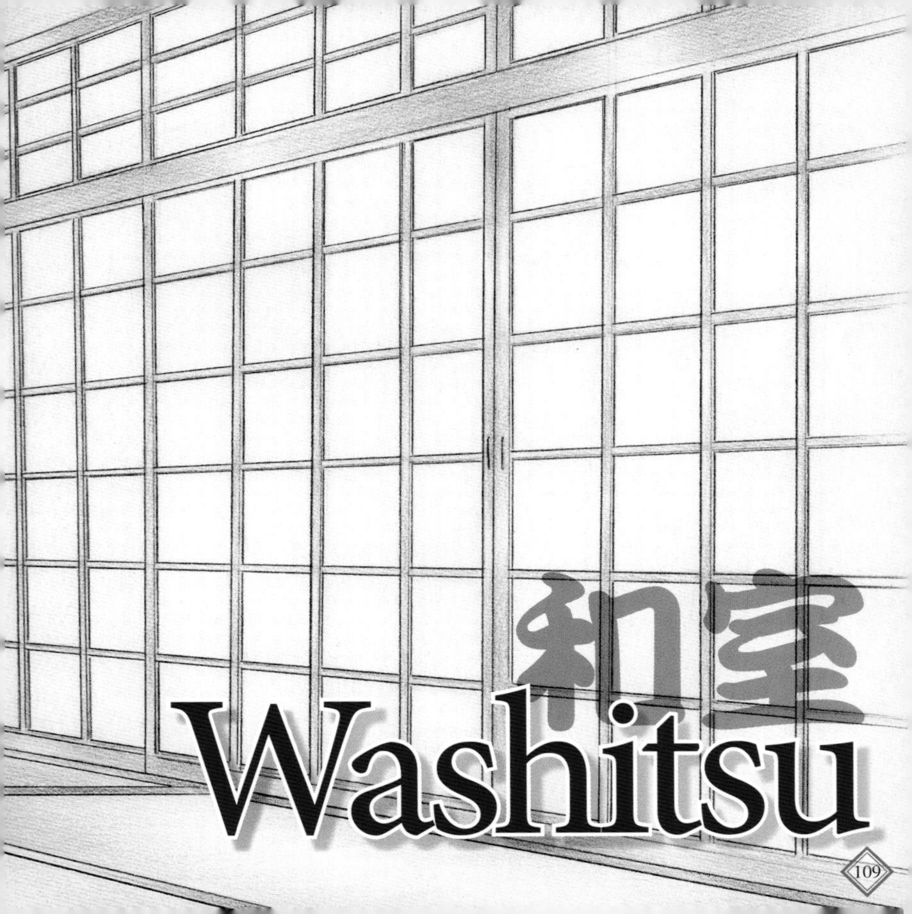

About the Artwork

All of the illustrations in this book were drawn by hand — quite unusual in this age of digital design. Here, using the *suika-wari* illustration from pages 86-87 as an example, we take a firsthand look at Atsuhisa Okura's unique artistic process. It can take him up to 30 days to achieve the proper color balance and complete a drawing.

1

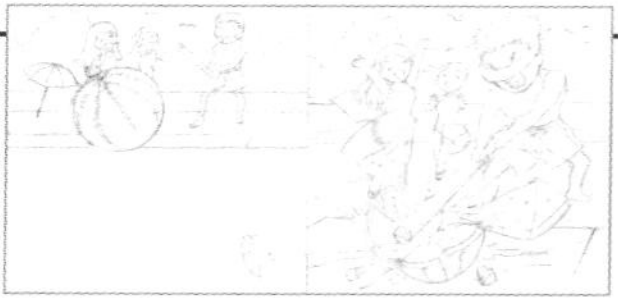

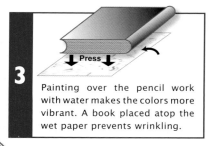

The rough sketch is drawn in pencil on inexpensive A4-size paper. Areas that will be shaded later are also sketched.

2

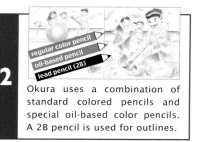

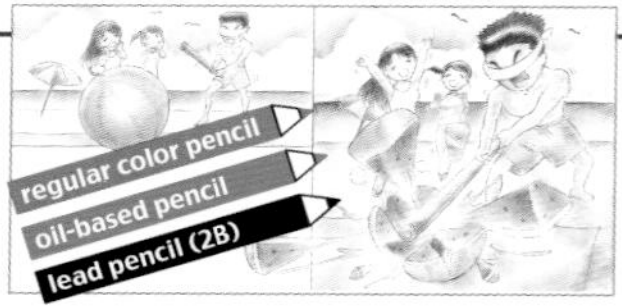
regular color pencil
oil-based pencil
lead pencil (2B)

Okura uses a combination of standard colored pencils and special oil-based color pencils. A 2B pencil is used for outlines.

3

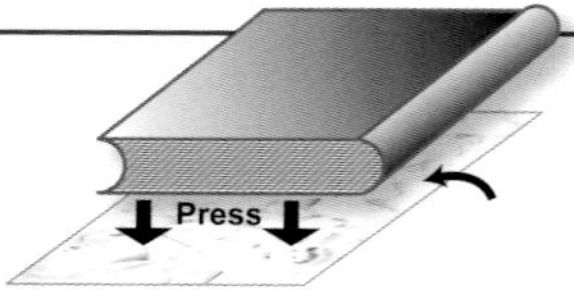
Press

Painting over the pencil work with water makes the colors more vibrant. A book placed atop the wet paper prevents wrinkling.

4

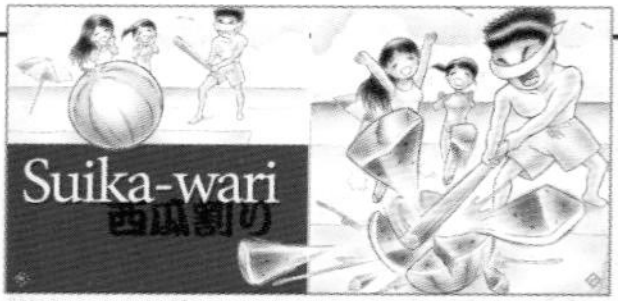
Suika-wari
西瓜割り

White correction fluid ink brings out certain highlights, such as the glow of the watermelon and the clouds on the horizon.

Layers of Colors

To call the artistic method Atsuhisa Okura uses to bring his illustrations to life "labor-intensive" is an understatement. It can take up to 30 days to complete a drawing measuring no more than 5 inches by 5 inches. Working up to 16 hours a day, seven days a week, he finished the drawings for this book in about four months.

A

B

C

D

Okura colors and then re-colors each drawing several times to achieve the desired look. And because he paints over the colored pencil with water, each drawing must dry for a day before the next layer of color can be added. This simplified view shows how the images come to life.

E

highlight
highlight

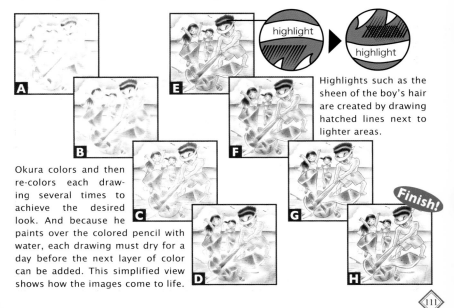

Highlights such as the sheen of the boy's hair are created by drawing hatched lines next to lighter areas.

F

G

Finish!
H

EDO KUROSAWA was born in the islands of southern Japan, where deadly snakes stalk the sugar cane fields and unspoiled beaches are never more than five minutes away. He was educated in the United States, where he vowed to become a bridge between the two cultures that earned his love and respect.

ATSUHISA OKURA is a Tokyo native whose manga stories have appeared in *Business Jump* and *Shonen Magazine,* among others. He is a past recipient of the prestigious Kodansha and Shueisha prizes for best new manga artist.

MANGA
UNIVERSITY®
Gift Books

ORDERING INFORMATION

Visit our campus store:
www.mangauniversity.com

Send us an email:
info@mangauniversity.com

Call us toll-free in the USA:
1-877-BUY-MANGA (877-289-6264)